1,077 WTF
Fun Facts
To Leave You In Disbelief

Charles Klotz

Cover design by: PixelStudio
Library of Congress Control Number:
2018675309
Printed in the United States of America

"Never give up on what you really want to do. The person with big dreams is more powerful than the one with all the facts."

-H. Jackson Brown, Jr.

CONTENTS

PREFACE

I hope you enjoy this list of 1,077 fun facts. For source
information on each of our facts or to explore more
interesting facts and fun images, head to our website
https://www.wtffunfact.com. There we have over 11,000
fun facts organized by category just waiting for you to
browse.

1,077 FUN FACTS

In the near future, you can spend up to 30 nights on the International Space Station for $35,000 per night (transportation not included). Wi-Fi is also extra but is a reasonable $50 per gigabyte.

***

The Argentine Football Association published a cultural manual ahead of the 2018 World Cup that included a section on how to seduce Russian women.

***

In Japanese culture, shaving your head is a common form of public apology or an acknowledgement of failure.

***

Actor Jonah Hill was hospitalized with bronchitis after snorting too much fake cocaine during the filming of The Wolf of Wall Street.

***

Prince Charles had engineers modify his Aston Martin Volante to run on biofuel made from white wine.

***

Laid end-to-end, an adult's arteries, veins and capillaries would stretch for about 100,000 miles - enough to wrap around the world nearly four times.

***

The first assassination attempt on Archduke Ferdinand failed spectacularly. The bomb bounced off the car and exploded under the wrong vehicle. The assassin then fled, diving into a nearby dry riverbed and eventually vomiting up his own suicide pill.

***

Researchers found that the price paid for something impacts the way we taste and enjoy it. For example, paying a lot more money for the same bottle of wine gives the drinker more pleasure because the higher price causes more blood and oxygen to be sent to the part of the brain responsible for feeling pleasure.

***

The "seeds" on the outside of the strawberry are not actually seeds but ovaries called achenes that contain a separate fruit with a single seed inside it.

***

A Chinese family adopted what they thought was a Tibetan mastiff but it turned out to be an Asiatic black bear instead.

***

In 14th century England, they baptized children with cider because it was cleaner than the water.

***

Urban Outfitters used to sell a board game called *Ghettopoly* with bonus cards that read: "You got yo whole neighborhood addicted to crack. Collect $50 from each playa."

***

Instant ramen was invented by Momofuku Ando in 1958 and was voted Japan's greatest invention of the 20th century by the Japanese.

***

The Sahara Desert is made of only 15% sand and sand dunes. Majority of the Sahara and other deserts is rock, rocky plateaus, and gravel covered plains. The sand is just a result of the wind eroding the rock.

***

A scientist at McMurdo Station in Antarctica used Tinder to find a match with a camper 45 miles away in the Dry Valleys. It's the first suspected match on that continent.

***

Clinique and Crayola have teamed up to create a box of lipstick crayons that are color-matched to actual Crayola shades.

***

The average energy expended during the ladies Wimbledon tennis final match adds up to 1.56kWh, which is enough power to keep an iPhone charged for a year.

***

Mississippi only ratified the 13th amendment, which abolished slavery back in 1865, in 1995. However, they never officially notified the US Archivist and so it had to be corrected and was finally ratified in 2013.

***

A 102-year-old German woman is the oldest to receive a PhD. She was banned from attending her final oral exam in 1938 by the Nazi influenced university because she was Jewish.

***

France passed a 'right to disconnect' law in 2017, allowing people to ignore emails that arrive outside business hours.

***

Latchkey incontinence is the increased feeling of "having to go" the closer you get to the restroom. It is a conditioned subconscious response similar to what Pavlov proved with his scientific experiment with his dog.

***

Aretha Franklin always insisted on being paid upfront and in cash before performances. She'd keep the cash with her security team or occasionally in her purse which she brought on stage.

***

In 2009, Saudi Arabia created a special "Anti-Witchcraft Unit" and a telephone hotline for the public to report magical misdeeds.

***

Father's Day is historically the busiest day for collect-calls, while Mother's Day is the busiest day for regular phone calls.

***

Dalmatians are the official firehouse dog because in the 18th century they would run alongside horse-drawn "fire engines" and prevent other dogs or animals from spooking the horses.

***

Pop star Madonna at one point worked at Dunkin' Donuts but was fired for squirting the customers with jam.

***

Parietal cells in your stomach produce hydrochloric acid which helps to break down food. This acid is so concentrated that one drop would eat straight through a piece of wood.

***

The Australian Rainbow Lorikeet routinely gets drunk on the fermented crimson flower nectar from the Weeping Boer-bean tree and make loud noises during spring and summer.

***

The most radioactive places at Chernobyl are no longer the #4 reactor area but the hospital room where they left all the first responders' clothes and the equipment they used to clean up all the debris from the explosion.

***

Pavarotti holds the record for curtain calls doing 165 after a performance of the Donizetti opera "L'elisir d'amore" at the Deutsche Oper Berlin in 1988.

***

Guns N' Roses guitarist Slash once walked in on his mother naked in bed with David Bowie.

***

Research in Canada has found that toddlers who learn how to lie early on are more likely to do better later in life. The study found only 1/5 of two-year-olds know how to lie.

***

The Turritopsis Dohrnii aka immortal jellyfish can live forever by transforming back into their juvenile polyp state after reproducing. They retract their tentacles, their bodies shrink, and they sink to the ocean floor and start the life cycle all over again. They only die by being eaten by a predator or contracting a disease.

***

Puffins are a local delicacy in Iceland. You can find them served smoked, grilled, or boiled.

***

Coco Chanel, the founder of fashion and perfume empire Chanel, was a nazi spy during WWII with the code name of 'Westminster' due to her connections with British high society.

***

Caffeine extracted from coffee beans to make decaf coffee is sold as crude caffeine to refiners and the pure caffeine is ultimately sold to soft drink makers like Coca Cola and Pepsi.

***

In 2009, a man was arrested in Ireland after Slovakian security placed explosives in his luggage for training purposes and forgot to remove them.

***

Adermatoglyphia, or immigration delay disease, is a genetic mutation that causes people to be born without fingerprints. Worldwide it affects only 4 known extended families.

***

Google's parent company Alphabet Inc.'s web address is abc.xyz.

***

The Election Commission of India sets up a polling station 25 miles inside the remote lion sanctuary of Gir Forest National Park so that a single person, the priest of a local temple, can vote.

***

One in four people have a hole in their heart called a Patent Foramen Ovale (PFO), which has been there since they were newborns.

***

In 2015, Snoop Dogg showed up 2 hours late for a concert in Haarlem, Netherlands and then proceeded to stream football on his laptop during the performance. He shared it all on his Instagram.

***

There are only two sets of escalators in the entire state of Wyoming.

***

The rules of golf at St. Andrews in 1812 state that if your ball strikes your adversary or their caddy then they lose the hole.

***

Around 2200 B.C., the Egyptians created the first synthetically created color blue. This Egyptian Blue color glows under fluorescent lights allowing historians to identify the color even when its not visible.

***

Thieves stole a small horn shark from the San Antonio Aquarium using a baby stroller to smuggle the shark out.

***

Research shows that you burn more calories taking a set of stairs a single step at a time instead of two at a time.

***

The ancient Egyptians, while under the rule of Ptolemy II, would confiscate any books that arrived on ships and make a copy. They would then keep the original in the library of Alexandria and return the copied version to the owner.

***

Americans spend an average of 37 minutes a day doing meal preparation and cleanup. This is roughly half the amount of time that was spent in the 1960's.

***

The 18th century word leint means to "urinate in an alcoholic beverage to increase its strength".

***

Australia's first police force (the Night Watch) was made up of 12 of the best-behaved criminals.

***

In 1941, Harvard University undergrad had an acceptance rate of 92%, compared to the 4.5% for the class of 2023.

***

The famous Star Trek phrase "Beam me up, Scotty!" was never actually said in any of the Star Trek films or television shows.

***

Americans eat 20 billion hot dogs annually, which is about 70 hot dogs per person. They are served in 95% of American homes.

***

There was an actual tree in La Jolla which inspired Dr. Seuss's Trufulla trees in his book The Lorax. The ~100-year-old Monterey Cypress unexpectedly fell over in June 2019.

***

The drug Viagra (or sildenafil) was originally intended to be a heart medication designed to treat angina by increasing blood flow to the heart, but it failed at that.

***

The skating brand Supreme's logo is ironically based on propaganda artist Barbara Kruger's anti-consumerism works.

***

King Tut is the only mummy from ancient Egypt known to have been mummified with an erection. His member subsequently broke off soon after the mummy was discovered.

***

Twenty percent of all marriages globally are between first cousins.

***

Retired Spanish cyclist Miguel Induráin had a resting heart rate of 28 beats per minute during his career. The normal range for people is 60 - 72 BPM.

***

In 2020, OceanGate will begin tours of the Titanic via their private submarine Titan at a cost of $125,000 per person.

***

The city of Vancouver has banned doorknobs on all new home construction. They must instead use levers.

***

There is a road in Sweden that charges electric cars as they drive on it. The project is called eRoadArlanda and works in rain or snow as well.

***

The Roncalli Circus in Germany has replaced live animal acts with holographs created by 11 specialized projectors displaying from multiple angles to create a flawless visual for all guests.

***

Up until 2008, the chemical TBT was used in ship's anti-fouling paint, which caused female snails to grow penises and ultimately explode because they couldn't shed their eggs.

***

The original word for bear has been lost because our ancient ancestors were so worried saying the name of the animal would cause it to come after them. Instead they used the term bruin, meaning the brown one, which then segued into bear.

***

There's a Swedish startup company called Cangaroo who want you to rent app-enabled pogo sticks to get around your city.

***

A 2011 study found that there is a genetic mutation in half the world's population which causes brussels sprouts to taste very bitter to them.

***

The original artist of Scooby-Doo, Iwao Takamoto, drew the Great Dane with features that are the exact opposite of what is considered desirable by breeders, including a hump back, bowed legs, and a small chin.

***

French artist, Gentil Garçon, worked with a paleontologist, François Escuilié, to create a skull of the pellet-gobbling video game icon, Pac Man.

***

The US has roughly 100,000 patients waiting for a kidney transplant and yet over 2,000 kidneys are discarded each year, 1/5th of them because a recipient couldn't be found.

***

The British monarch celebrates two birthdays, one on their actual birthday and then officially in the summer when the weather is nice enough for a parade.

***

A missing Indonesian woman was found clothed and entirely intact when local villagers dissected a 23-foot-long reticulated python.

***

Piranha soup is a popular dish and considered an aphrodisiac in Brazil.

***

Playing the electronic song 'Scary Monsters and Nice Sprites' by Skrillex reduces mosquito bites and also hinders their ability to mate.

***

The original 'friendship tree' between US President Trump and French President Macron died in quarantine once uprooted after the ceremonial planting. Macron is sending a replacement oak tree.

***

Before refrigerators, Russians and Finns would put live brown frogs in their milk to keep it from spoiling.

***

The wreck of the RMS Titanic was found during the Cold War as part of a secret US Naval investigation of two sunken nuclear submarines. The Navy never expected the oceanographer to actually find the Titanic.

***

A Texas man was sentenced to 50 years in jail for stealing $1.2 million worth of fajitas.

***

The national bird of Peru is the Andean cock-of-the-rock.

***

Juan Pujol García was a rogue spy during WWII. Britain's MI5 declined his offer to be their spy and he went and spied on Germany anyways as a double agent. He lived in Lisbon and made up an elaborate network of fictional agents and reports based on tourist guides and other public sources. He is one of the only people to be awarded a medal by both the Axis and Allies.

***

There's an iPhone app to detect a ripe watermelon. You repeatedly knock on the fruit with phone's microphone nearby and it analyzes the sound.

***

The Big Dipper which makes up part of the constellation Ursa Major is known as The Plough in the UK and Le Casserole in France.

***

There's a persistent lava lake in Mount Michael, a volcano on Saunders Island in the Antarctic, which has been there since at least 2003.

***

In 2012, at a pop-up shop in London's St. Bart's Pathology Museum, STD decorated cupcakes were showcased in an effort to promote safe sex. The cupcakes feature scabs, boils, green-colored genital discharge and warts.

***

Marie Curie, the first woman to win a Nobel Prize and first person to win two, wasn't legally allowed to attend college as a woman. Instead, she attended the secret Polish Flying University.

***

Before Edgar Allen Poe sold his poem The Raven for $9, or roughly $300 in today's dollars, to The American Review, the owner of Graham's Magazine gifted him $15 after turning Poe down because he thought the poem was a cry for help.

***

John Willis is one of only a few white members in Ping On, Boston's Chinese mafia. He was introduced to the group by a young Asian man he defended. John later learned Chinese, became the boss's chief bodyguard, and received the nickname "White Devil". He is currently in a federal prison for drug trafficking.

***

A Ugandan man saw his father lose their land in a legal fight at age 6. He spent 18 years in school and became a lawyer and won back the land 23 years later.

***

Glossy magazines are radioactive. They are made with a white clay called kaolin which contains elevated levels of uranium and thorium.

***

Cats have a dominant paw very similar to how humans have a dominant hand. These preferences also differ by sex - same as in humans. Males tend to prefer their left paws, whereas females were more likely to be righties.

***

A mouse's sperm is much, much larger than an elephant's sperm. However, the fruit fly produces the longest sperm known to science.

***

A 74-year-old Japanese man dressed as a ninja and burgled 254 homes and stole $260,000 worth of goods before finally being caught by local police.

***

The Miracle Berry, or synsepalum dulcificum, is a fruit from West Africa which contains the taste modifier Miraculin. When you eat the fruit, the miraculin molecules bind to the tongue causing sour foods to taste sweet.

***

Umami is the recently identified fifth taste. It is described as a savory flavor and is caused by glutamate, an amino acid. It is associated with foods like tomatoes, meat, cheese, mushrooms, and more.

***

There is a Wait Calculation for interstellar travel. It attempts to determine the minimum number of years it should take us to travel somewhere, such that a future mission doesn't pass the previous one due to advances in propulsion technology.

***

Penn & Teller created a video game in 1995 called 'Desert Bus'. In the game, the player drives an 8-hour bus route in real time between Tucson and Vegas. The scenery never changes from rocks and road signs and once the player reaches the destination, they have to turn around and drive back.

***

The amniotic fluid in a mother's womb, which can be nearly a liter of fluids at 30+ weeks, is replaced every 3 hours towards the end of pregnancy.

***

The band Foo Fighters started with just Dave Grohl alone playing all the instruments and singing all the vocals. He hoped the name would keep him anonymous and make people think there were multiple band members. He now thinks it's a terrible name.

***

There's a book called 'Fat Brad The Cookbook'. It is based on all the foods that actor Brad Pitt has eaten in his movies.

***

J.R.R. Tolkien was nominated by fellow author CS Lewis for the 1961 Nobel Prize in Literature, but was overlooked because the jury said the quality of his storytelling wasn't good enough.

***

In molecular physics, there is a principle called Van der Waals Forces, which are the tiny attractive forces between atoms and molecules. This is what allows geckos to stick to and climb almost anything.

***

Thomas Jefferson helped popularize mac and cheese in America by serving it to his dinner guests during his Presidency. He even had his own recipe.

***

Starting in 1948, a man wore giant 3-toed lead shoes and stomped around Florida beaches, leading locals to believe there was a giant penguin inhabiting the area. He did this randomly for the next 10 years. The prankster finally revealed himself and his shoes 40 years later.

***

The made-up name of Khaleesi from George R. R. Martin's 'A Song of Ice and Fire' novels only became popular after HBO's release of Game of Thrones. In 2012, 146 babies were named Khaleesi in the US.

***

The term decimate's original definition was "to kill one in 10". The practice was used by the Roman army in the fifth century BC as a way to inspire fear and loyalty. If any of a cohort's soldiers acted cowardly or deserted, then lots were drawn and one unlucky soldier out of every 10 in that cohort would be killed by their own comrades.

***

There is a group of sea wolves on Vancouver Island that can swim for miles and 90% of their diet is seafood. They primarily eat salmon but also forage on barnacles, lams, herring eggs, seals, and river otters.

***

Ruth Wakefield was the original creator of the chocolate-chip cookie. She sold the recipe for the Toll House Chocolate Crunch Cookie to Nestlé for one dollar and a lifetime supply of chocolate.

***

In 2012, a designer from Georgia created a fake Louis Vuitton condom and sold them for $68 apiece.

***

Three seals were trained to copy sounds which subsequently resulted in them performing a several-note rendition of Star Wars and Twinkle Twinkle Little Star.

***

There is a colorless and odorless liquid you can breathe in which is called perfluorohexane. Animals can be submerged in it without drowning.

***

Despite some broader urban legends, studies how Polar bears are the only type of bears known to be attracted to women menstruating.

***

An inflatable of the famous "Tank Man" was put in Taiwan to mark the anniversary of Tiananmen Protests in Beijing, China.

***

Wheelchair athletes with spinal injuries would intentionally injure the lower part of their body to increase their blood pressure which would enhance their performance. This practice is called 'Boosting' and has been banned by the International Paralympic Committee since 1994.

***

The self-explanatory 'new car smell' is a result of the 200+ chemical compounds (some of them toxic) found in cars being unstable and prone to off-gassing, or releasing chemical vapors, which leads to the odor we all know and love.

***

There is a website called PointerPointer.com that will match a picture of people pointing fingers at your cursor.

***

The first fireworks were created as a result of the ancient Chinese's quest for immortality. In early-ninth-century China, alchemy was practiced in order to produce a substance that would prolong life.

***

Human composting, an alternative to traditional burying and cremation, will become legal in Washington state starting May 1, 2020.

***

The non-stick coating called Teflon, or polytetrafluoroethylene, was accidentally invented by Roy Plunkett while trying to create a new refrigerant.

***

Hundreds of tiny islands, known as crannogs, around Scotland are actually man made and were constructed out of boulders, clay and timbers by Neolithic people about 5,600 years ago.

***

A 1700-year-old baobab tree in Modjadjiskloof, South Africa had a 15-person full bar inside its 155-foot-wide trunk called the Big Baobab Tree Bar. The bar closed and the tree eventually fell over in 2017.

***

Ancient people in China practiced human head-shaping about 12,000 years ago. They bound growing children's skulls in order to create a more elongated and oval shape. The reasoning and purpose of this practice is still unknown.

***

There is over 4 million cubic yards of concrete in the Hoover Dam and power plant, which is enough to build a highway from the East coast to the West coast of the US.

***

There is only one single stop sign in Paris, France, which is located in the 16th arrondissement.

***

From 007 movies Dr. No to Quantum of Solace, James Bond has killed 352 people and slept with 52 women.

***

A new alternative cancer treatment is being researched and involves injecting dead cells into the body. Preliminary studies show injecting dying cells into tumors helps the immune cells target the cancer.

***

A 2013 study found that men who are wealthy prefer women with smaller breasts while men who are less financially secure prefer larger.

***

The middle finger has been used as a derogatory gesture for at least 2400 years, appearing in ancient Greek and Roman texts. Its usage in the US is documented as early as 1886 and was likely brought over by Italian immigrants.

***

There are over 40 million prostitutes in the world and over a million in the USA despite it being legalized only in Nevada. 80% of prostitutes are female.

***

If you remove a fruit fly's front legs, which contain a number of sensory organs, then it will mate with both male and female fruit flies as well as other fly species.

***

Carlos "White Feather" Hathcock was a legendary Vietnam War sniper who crawled for 3 days across 2000m of open field, killed a general with one shot, and then crawled back. He had over 93 confirmed kills, one from over 2500 yards away.

***

In 1905, the Cullinan Diamond (the largest, gem-quality rough diamond ever found) was supposedly sent from South Africa to the United Kingdom by a heavily guarded steamboat. In actuality, they mailed it in a plain box using registered post.

***

Ioannis Ikonomou works as a translator for the European Commission, speaking 21 of the 24 EU official languages. He can speak a total of 47 languages including many dead languages like Old Church Slavic.

***

Palm trees are not trees at all and belong to the grass family. Botanists define trees as woody plants with secondary growth. Palms lack both of these. They create their tough, "wood" epidermis through primary thickening and lignification.

***

The seven sins according to Gandhi: "Wealth without work. Pleasure without conscience. Knowledge without character. Commerce without morality. Science without humanity. Religion without sacrifice. Politics without principle."

***

The summit of Mt. Everest is made of marine limestone which means the highest point on earth was once at the bottom of the sea.

***

A 900 lb. Mako shark was once autopsied and found to have two pugnose eels living inside its heart chambers.

***

In 2007, Navy SEAL Mike Day was shot 27 times by three al-Qaeda gunman and knocked unconscious by a grenade. When he awoke, he managed to kill two of them and escape to the extraction helicopter. He has now recovered and is participating in Ironman competitions.

***

Some baby turtles talk to each other while they are still in their eggs so that they all hatch together.

***

There's a maximum-security prison in Uganda with its own soccer league. They have 10 formal teams, a governing body (the UPSA), and tournaments which feature prizes such as sugar, soap, and goats.

***

There are only 3 human beings that have died outside Earth's atmosphere. They are the three cosmonauts who died aboard the Soyuz 11 in 1971.

***

There's a fiction-based religion called Snapeism which has Snapewives or Snapeists who channel Snape, are in romantic relationships with him, and use him as a guide for their daily lives.

***

Horror writer Stephen King sleeps with his lights on. King admitted to sleeping with the lights on back in 1982 when he was just really getting started in his career.

***

Ichiro Suzuki, baseball's all-time hits leader, learned Spanish just for the purpose of trash talking opponents.

***

Cocktails became popular during Prohibition because juices were needed to hide the taste of some of the ingredients in the moonshine like dead rats, rotten meat, wood tar, and others.

***

The sea squirt starts as an egg, develops into a tadpole of sorts, then attaches itself to an object - boat hull, rocks, ocean floor and doesn't move again. It then consumes its own brain as it is longer required.

***

In 1983, a 61-year-old potato farmer Cliff Young won the inaugural Sydney to Melbourne Ultramarathon in overall and work boots.

***

Dr. Seuss cheated on his wife while she had cancer. After finding out about the affair, she killed herself and Dr. Seuss married his mistress.

***

Sea otters have loose skin across their chest which creates a pouch for them to store rocks and food. They use the rocks to help them crack open shellfish and clams.

***

In 2008, Dmitry Agarkov scanned in a credit card agreement he had received with much higher interest rates than advertised and changed all the terms to show 0% interest and no fees. The bank unknowingly signed and approved it and a judge later upheld the contract. -

***

A swarm of 20,000 bees once followed a car for two days because their queen was trapped inside the car.

***

In 2015, a Chinese billionaire bought a US$170 million painting by with his credit card so he could use the points for free airfare.

***

After visiting the Caribbean and seeing beer bottles littered all over the beaches in 1963, Alfred Heineken created a square beer bottle that could double as a brick to build homes in impoverished countries.

***

If the Ancient Persians decided something while drunk, they had a rule to reconsider it when sober. If they made a decision sober, they would reconsider it while drunk.

***

Octopuses have many neurons in their tentacles such that a severed tentacle can continue reacting to stimuli even after they are no longer connected to the main brain. If you put food near a severed tentacle it will even try to feed it to a mouth that's not there.

***

Mississippi is the only state that allows you to drink alcohol while driving, so long as your blood alcohol content level stays below the legal limit.

***

Blockbuster had the chance to buy Netflix for US$50 million in 2000 but turned it down to go into business with Enron.

***

In 2019, the grasshopper swarm that invaded Las Vegas, Nevada was so bad that it appeared on weather radar.

***

In 2019, DNA tests revealed the Dutch fertility doctor Jan Karbaat inseminated 49 patients with his own sperm.

***

A dog's sense of smell is 100,000 times stronger than a human's. Bloodhounds have ~300 million scent receptors while beagles and German shepherds both have ~225 million. In comparison, humans only have about 5 million.

***

An acersecomic is a person who has never had a haircut in their life.

***

Helium (He) is the only element on the periodic table that was not discovered on Earth. It was found when analyzing the sun's spectrum, hence its name which comes from the Greek god of the sun Helios.

***

South African scientists detected traces of Cannabis on pipes found in William Shakespeare's garden.

***

Starting life underwater, in tough times the Rocky Mountain tiger salamander can resort to cannibalism and even seal its gills and grow lungs to live on land.

***

After initially being declined by the government, Civil War commander John T. Wilder and his soldiers took out personal loans to purchase Spencer repeating rifles at $35 each. The government eventually paid for the rifles to avoid embarrassment.

***

Disney has credited their coffee guy in 8 of their films, including Zootopia and Frozen.

***

Californian-based artist Hoang Tran makes intricate crayon carvings of famous characters from pop culture. Each hand-carved sculpture takes several hours to complete.

***

A New York City man was exonerated and released, after being held in jail for transporting child pornography, when porn star Lupe Fuentes flew from Spain to appear at his trial with her ID and passport proving her age.

***

In 1987, a man convinced 2.8 million people to send him a penny each for his college education.

***

History and prehistory are marked by the invention of records. Anything before written record is 'prehistory' and any records are in 'history'.

***

The vending machines in Japan are set to dispense drinking water for free if the water supply gets cut off during a disaster.

***

Two guys used their dead friend's ashes as fishing bait and caught the words biggest carp.

***

If you pick up two objects at the same time that have the same weight but are different sizes, the larger object will seem lighter. This phenomenon is known as the Size-Weight Illusion.

***

In certain countries, like Belgium, Austria, Mexico, and Germany, there is no additional time added to one's sentence for attempting to and escaping prison, because they believe it is human nature to want to escape.

***

Instead of "Once upon a time," many Korean folktales begin with "Back when tigers used to smoke..."

***

A drug trafficker, nicknamed 'Shorty', was caught trying to escape a Rio de Janeiro jail by dressing up as his teenage daughter, who was scheduled to visit him that day.

***

Operation Tracer was a secret backup plan in case the Axis ever captured Gibraltar during WWII. Six men would be sealed in a secret cave overlooking the harbor and report back enemy movements. There were enough supplies to last for 7 years.

***

Uber's first CEO, Ryan Graves, was an unpaid intern at Foursquare, who got hired after he answered a job listing on Twitter. He's now worth billions.

***

There is a DIY Netflix Project to create a "Netflix and Chill" button. Dubbed The Switch, when you activate it, the lights dim, your phone is set to do-not-disturb, food is ordered for delivery, and Netflix is readied for streaming.

***

The 'Tall Boy', as the crazy, arm-flailing, inflatable tube characters were originally known as, was invented by carnival artist Peter Minshall for the 1996 Olympic games in Atlanta.

***

Soccer star Cristiano Ronaldo refuses to get any tattoos on his body just so he can continue on donating blood.

***

Chef Josh Niland has created a fish turducken. His seafood version features yellowfin tuna loin, wrapped in a cod fillet, wrapped in an enormous tail-on ocean trout fillet. The entire recipe will cost you roughly $250.

***

The Game Of Thrones season 8 premiere was pirated nearly 55 million times in a single day.

***

If a self-driving car gets in an accident that is clearly its fault, then the owner doesn't pay damages - the manufacturers do.

***

A London commuter received a settlement of over $32,000 from Network Rail after they "possibly" slipped on pigeon poop at Paddington train station.

***

In an effort to reduce car accidents involving elderly drivers, a Japanese restaurant is offering a 10% discount at a ramen restaurant if they hand in their driver's license.

***

The hit TV show Stranger Things was rejected 15 to 20 times by different networks before Netflix finally picked it up.

***

Goldfish will lose their color and turn white if they are kept in the dark and not exposed to any sunlight.

***

Brazilian electronics company Gradiente is legally allowed to sell their 'iPhone' because they trademarked it back in 2000. The phone uses an Android operating system.

***

In 1939, Adolf Hitler's nephew wrote an article that was published in Look Magazine called "Why I Hate My Uncle."

***

GE is to blame for your elders warning you not to sit too close to the TV. In 1967, they manufactured a color TV which emitted excessive radiation due to a "factory error"□. GE fixed the problem going forward by putting a leaded glass shield around the tubes.

***

When Prince died in 2016, he did not leave a will for his estate worth hundreds of millions of dollars. Within three weeks of his death, nearly 700 people claimed to be his half-sibling in hopes of cashing in on his death. As of 2019, his estate has still not been settled.

***

A US study found that the more money you make, the less time you spend on the internet. Wealth also predicts the type of websites visited.

***

There is a litigation defense strategy used by authors when defaming people dubbed 'the small penis rule'. The author, when describing a character, will add that they have a small penis, assuming that nobody would sue them for libel and admit to having a small penis.

***

A check in the US does not need to be written on a specific bank check paper. A check can be written on

***

A Mongolian couple believed a folk remedy and consumed raw marmot meat and organs to improve their health. They ended up contracting

***

A 2014 study found that having a glass or two of wine before a meal caused people to eat nearly 25% more food during the meal.

***

For 4 years, Hugh Grant was his own talent agent under the made-up name of James Howe Ealy. He would speak with a fake Scottish accent when on the phone. He claims to have saved himself a fortune while doing so.

***

The ozone layer above Antarctica is showing signs of healing, thanks to the worldwide ban on chlorofluorocarbons. The hole in the ozone may fully heal by 2080.

***

A leech has both male and female organs. In total they have 18 testicles and 2 ovaries. They also have 32 brains and 10 stomachs.

***

Squirrels were originally a purposeful introduction into urban American cities in the mid 1800's. They were meant to remind city inhabitants of nature and feel "rural peace and calm".

***

The U.S. military spent over US$20 billion a year on air conditioning in Iraq and Afghanistan. That's more than NASA's budget.

***

The Dutch crown jewels include a coronation crown that is not meant to be worn, which is made of fake pearls, fish scales, and some colored foil.

***

According to the Pentagon, 71% of Americans between the ages of 17 and 24 are ineligible to join the military. They are too overweight, too poorly educated, or have a criminal record.

***

Post-relationship grief affects men, in the long term, more than women.

***

Saint George is the patron saint of England and a few other places, but he is also the patron saint of skin disease sufferers including lepers and leprosy as well as syphilitic people and syphilis.

***

China has created a social credit score system for dog owners. You lose points for no leash, not cleaning up poop, or any other disturbance reports. Once you lose 12 points, you will temporarily lose your dog until you pass a test on pet policy.

***

Aitzaz Hassan, a 15-years-old, Pakistani schoolboy, who in 2014, when he saw a suicide bomber at the gates to his school, decided to confront the man, while his friends ran inside, detonating the bomb, and saving upwards of 2000 children.

***

Without its smell, coffee would have only a sour or bitter taste due to the organic acids. You can test this by holding your nose as you take a sip.

***

In 2010, Finland was the first country in the world to make broadband internet (>1Mbps) a legal right for each of its citizens.

***

Spiders can get high and build very different kinds of webs while on weed, caffeine, mescaline and LSD.

***

A large cigarette-smoking, beer-drinking bear named Wojtek was enlisted in the Polish army during WWII. He was promoted to a corporal after his efforts during the battle of Monte Cassino.

***

Contestants on Jeopardy! are not allowed to bet $69, $666, $14, $88, or $1488 during final Jeopardy.

***

Kobe Bryant has the most missed shots in NBA history (14,481) but still averaged 25.4 points per game over his 19 years in the NBA, shooting 45.3% from the floor and making 33% of his career three-pointers.

***

The Ancient Romans used powdered mouse brains for toothpaste. They flavored it with charcoal and bark.

***

Magician Harry Houdini took a year off from his performance career during WWI to promote the war effort including teaching soldiers how to get out of handcuffs.

***

A 25-year-old Kenyan man invented smart gloves that can convert sign language movements into speech.

***

The FDA allows heavy metals like lead, arsenic, and mercury in cosmetics like lipstick and eye shadows.

***

A German shepherd named Talero stayed next to the body of his owner for 23 days after he had died in a snow storm. He prevented animals from attacking the body and tried to keep his owner warm by sleeping by his side.

***

Voice actress Dionne Quan, who voiced Trixie Trang in Fairly Odd Parents and Kimi in Rugrats, is legally blind and all her acting scripts are written in braille.

***

The sun loses about 6 million tons of mass every second due to nuclear fusion and the solar wind. Despite constantly losing large sums of mass, it has only lost roughly 0.05% of its original mass over the last 4.5 billion years.

***

A couple from Paraguay moved in together in 1933. After 80 years, 8 children and 50 grandchildren, the 103-year-old man married his 99-year-old bride.

***

Pope John Paul II nominated Saint Isidore of Seville, a Bishop and Scholar, as the patron saint of the internet because he tried to record everything that was known in his 20 book opus Etymologies/Origins.

***

Male model Stefan-Pierre Tomlin aka "Mr. Tinder" received a record-breaking 14,600 matches in two years. After five years of swiping and matching nearly 20 women a day on the app, he finally found a girlfriend offline via a blind date.

***

A Volvo engineer invented and patented the three-point seatbelt in 1959. As a new safety measure, it was so significant that they opened up the patent to other automakers to help save lives instead of trying to profit from it.

***

Nazca Lines are located in Peru and were created by the ancient Nazca culture in South America. The 2,000-year-old Lines depict various plants, animals, and shapes and must be viewed from an above to be fully appreciated.

***

There is a period during Earth's evolution where activity stalled which scientists dubbed 'the boring billion'. Beginning roughly 1.7 billion years ago, the Earth became a slimy, near-static world of algae and microbes.

***

Pencils are typically yellow because the best graphite came from China in the 19th century. Creative pencil manufacturers began to color their pencils yellow (a royal color in Chinese culture) to indicate their high quality and associate them with China.

***

A recent study found that men on Tinder do not appear to be intimidated by highly educated women. They indicated interest in fictitious profiles with a Master's degree more often than those with a Bachelor's degree.

***

To avoid exciting men while riding, early bicycles had a cherry screen which hid women's ankles from view.

***

Freddy Krueger is an Amazonian parrot that found its way back to a Brazilian zoo after it was stolen by armed thieves after recently being shot and bitten by a snake.

***

A mysterious underground structure found in Russia near the Naryn-Kala citadel was identified as one of the oldest churches on Earth.

***

In 1763, the first dinosaur bone discovered was given the very descriptive and scientific name of Scrotum humanum by Richard Brookes. It later was identified as part of the femur of a Megalosaurus.

***

A recent study found people who eat spicy foods tend to live longer. Consumption of hot red chili peppers is associated with a 13% reduction in total mortality - primarily in deaths due to heart disease or stroke.

***

Movie theatre popcorn has an average markup of over 1200% percent. A bag of popcorn costs roughly $.37 and can sell for upwards of $5.

***

The record for the most kids born to a single mother is 69. Russian Valentina Vassilyeva labored 27 times and gave birth to 16 pairs of twins, 7 sets of triplets, and 4 sets of quadruplets.

***

A seven-year-old Indian boy complaining of jaw pain was treated in a local hospital and found to have 526 teeth inside his mouth.

***

The numbers on a roulette wheel when added together sum up to 666.

***

Contrary to what was depicted in the Jurassic Park movie franchise, velociraptors were no bigger in size than turkeys.

***

Asphalt pavements are America's most recycled product. Reclaimed asphalt pavement can be reused to make as high or higher quality pavement the next time. It can be recycled repeatedly and neither the aggregate nor the cement loses utility.

***

A 13-year-old opened a hot dog stand in front of his home in Minnesota, causing a complaint to the health department. Instead of shutting him down, the inspectors helped him bring his stand up to code and paid the $87 fee for his permit out of their own pockets. He now sells nearly 150 hot dogs a day.

***

McDonald's Chicken McNuggets come in four official shapes: bell, bone, boot, and ball.

***

During WWI, there was limited supplies of cotton, so doctors used sphagnum moss for bandages. It can hold 22x its own weight in liquid and is a natural antiseptic.

***

There is an action park in Minnesota which allows you to drive military tanks and other army vehicles, smash junk cars, shoot machine guns and drive through trailer houses.

***

In 2000, the table tennis federation voted to increase the diameter of the ping pong ball from 38mm to 40mm to make it easier to learn and make the sport better for TV. It was the first major change to the sport since 1937.

***

A man took his girlfriend on a tough, twisty 15-mile bicycling path that spelled out "marry me" when she checked her GPS map at the end of their ride.

***

Alex Trebek didn't take a single sick day for the first 34 years of Jeopardy! He hosted over 6,800 episodes and holds the world record for most game show episodes hosted by the same presenter.

***

The Sabre-Toothed Tiger or Smilodon was not actually a tiger or at all related to tigers or modern-day cats.

***

Joseph Medicine Crow earned the title 'War Chief' by completing four tasks as a warrior during WWII: leading a successful war party on a raid, capturing an enemy's weapon, touching an enemy without killing him, and stealing an enemy's horse.

***

A carpenter in Iowa named Dale Schroeder decided to donate his life savings to help local poor students go to college. In the 14 years since his death, his $3 million donation has sent 33 students to college on a full scholarship.

***

During the Ottoman Empire a 'batman' was a unit of weight equivalent to the modern day 7 lb. and 5 ounces.

***

Every year, Walt Disney World's Lost and Found collects more than 6,000 cell phones, 3,500 digital cameras, and 18,000 hats.

***

Ethan Zuckerman, inventor of the pop-up ad, has apologized to the world for creating one of the Internet's most hated forms of advertising.

***

A Scottish sailor named Alexander Selkirk was stranded on a deserted island in 1704, but survived for over 4 years, in part because feral cats protected him from the ravenous rats that attacked during the night.

***

Michael Myers, the killer from the Halloween movie franchise, wore a Captain Kirk mask spray painted white.

***

During a feud in 2009, the mayors of two neighboring Parisian suburbs each declared the same street one-way, but in opposite directions - resulting in chaos. The national police were called in to assist.

***

Benjamin Franklin created a pulley system so he could lock and unlock his bedroom door from his bed.

***

The Australian Great Barrier Reef is under attack by venomous sea stars known as crown-of-thorns starfish. Scientists created a robot called RangerBot to shoot them with bile.

***

In countries with poor identification document utilization or standardization, electoral ink (aka indelible ink) is used to prevent voter fraud. The silver nitrate in the ink can stain the skin for up to a couple weeks.

***

The South Korean boy band BTS was responsible for adding $3.6 billion to the local economy and accounted for one in every 13 tourist visits to the country in 2018. "

***

In 1981, a California doctor saved the life of a 3.2 lb. preemie baby boy. 30 years later, that doctor was involved in a car accident with a semi-truck and was saved by that baby, who became a paramedic.

***

Elephants have 3x as many neurons as humans have, but nobody knows why this doesn't result in them being smarter than us.

***

During the Elizabethan Age in England, people used mice to treat a number of ailments including whooping cough, measles, and smallpox. They would even cut them in half and apply it to warts to remove them.

***

Jim Carrey's portrayal of Lloyd in 'Dumb and Dumber' showcases Carrey's actual chipped front tooth, which is the result of a childhood fight. He has a cap which he removed for filming.

***

A Cleveland Browns football fan obituary requested six Cleveland Browns pallbearers at his funeral so "the Browns could let him down one last time".

***

Babies are born without knee caps. The cartilage begins to ossify and form the knee cap between 2 and 6 years of age.

***

Microwave doors have a metal mesh window to prevent the harmful microwaves from escaping. The holes are big enough to see inside but small enough to contain the microwaves.

***

When Salvador Dali was asked if he did drugs, he said "I don't do drugs... I am drugs."

***

There is a monument to the lab mouse in Siberia, Russia, commemorating their role in genetic research.

***

Bill Gates created his school's class scheduling program and he ensured he was placed in English class with mostly female students.

***

Beyonce was asked to perform at an Uber conference in Las Vegas in 2015. In lieu of a $6 million cash payment, she asked for equity in Uber. Uber IPO'd recently for $8.1 billion.

***

Thomas Jefferson bred and raised a special type of geese in order to supply himself with quill pens.

***

Robert Kearns invented intermittent windshield wipers and tried to sell his idea to the auto industry but was turned away. They soon began showing up on new cars, so he sued, and won.

***

Farmers will often put goldfish in their horse's water trough to eat the insects and prevent mosquito larvae from producing.

***

A full human cadaver for research costs roughly $500.

***

Quirkyalone is a term for people who enjoy being alone and single while waiting for the right person, instead of casually dating.

***

A recent study found that squirrels listen to the chatter of birds and respond accordingly. When birds' chirps were relaxed, then the squirrels relaxed. The opposite was also true, when the bird chatter was alarmed, the squirrels became more alert and vigilant.

***

Maurice Sendak's classic Where The Wild Things Are was originally titled Where The Wild Horses Are but Maurice realized he was unable to draw horses.

***

Farmers in the US are hacking their John Deere tractors with Ukrainian firmware purchased from invitation-only online forums in order to be able to have them serviced independently.

***

Nikola Tesla was able to perform integral calculus in his head, which often lead his teachers to believe he was cheating.

***

There are over 100 words in Hawaiian that are made up of only vowels.

***

Ray Lewis grew up using a deck of cards to do push-ups and sit-ups. If he drew a 7, he would do 7. An Ace was 25 and a Joker 30. He would go through the whole deck. During his NFL career, he would do it 3 times for each exercise.

***

In the hours before he was assassinated, Martin Luther King Jr. started a pillow fight in the hotel room with other civil rights leaders.

***

A Singapore Airlines cargo flight had to make an emergency landing in Bali due to a smoke sensor being triggered from the dung and farts of the 2,186 sheep aboard the plane.

***

Facebook co-founder Eduardo Saverin renounced his U.S. citizenship to avoid paying US$700 million in taxes.

***

A large part of the Māori culture is missing from recorded history because wet plate photography used by European settlers did not capture their unique Tā moko tattoos.

***

Woody Allen has only ever used an early 1950's manual Olympia SM-3 typewriter that he purchased when he was 16. Every script, screenplay, or comedy sketch was written on this one typewriter.

***

All of McDonald's delivery trucks in the UK have been running on used cooking oil from their restaurants since 2007.

***

Finnish soldier Aimo Koivunen overdosed on amphetamines while escaping Soviet forces during WWII. After regaining consciousness, he skied more than 250 miles, survived a land mine, and lay in a ditch for a week eating only pine buds and a raw bird. When he was rescued, his heart rate was still over 200 bpm and he weighed only 94 lb.

***

Mars' Snickers candy bar is the top selling candy bar in the world with over $2 billion in sales in 2016. It was named after the Mars family's favorite horse.

***

A convicted deer poacher in Missouri has been sentenced to watch Disney movie Bambi once a month for the entirety of his year-long sentence.

***

The Aztec's created a whistle in the shape of skulls called a death whistle. It produces a horrifying sound but its exact purpose is unknown. Experts think they may have been used during battle or as part of sacrificial ceremonies.

***

Over 12.5 million plastic rings were made in order to fabricate chain mail for the Lord of The Rings movie. Two crew members linked the rings by hand into suits of armor. By the end, they had worn their fingerprints off of their thumbs and index fingers.

***

Colorado has over 300 ghost towns, which is more than the number of active municipalities today. Many of them are old mining towns or mill towns that were abandoned in the 1890s.

***

Joseph "Moondyne Joe" Johns escaped prison so often that a special prison was built for him. The jailer was so confident in the new jail he promised to set Joe free if he ever escaped. Joe escaped and was caught 2 years later, but the jailer kept his word and freed him.

***

Saddam Hussein commissioned a calligrapher to write a copy of the Qur'an using vials of Saddam's blood. It took over two years and is known as the Blood Qur'an.

***

Peter Mayhew had the option to play either Chewbacca or Darth Vader when they were casting Star Wars. He wanted to be a hero and chose to play the 200-year-old hairy, yelling, Wookie.

***

High quality lenses made of rock-crystal were found among Viking artifacts. They are so well-made that they could be used in a telescope. They were crafted nearly 1,000 years ago.

***

Alexander Graham Bell, the inventor of the telephone, was also fascinated with breeding sheep with extra nipples after he purchased some land that came with a flock of sheep.

***

There are ~150 wallabies living in the forest of Rambouillet near Paris, France. They are descendants of several wallabies that escaped from the local zoo in the 1970's.

***

In 2015, three inmates from a maximum-security prison beat Harvard's debate team in a competitive debate arranged by the Bard College Prison Initiative.

***

The party game of Twister was originally called Pretzel, but Milton Bradley changed the name in 1965 due to trademark issues.

***

The specially created NASA Space Pen is used instead of a simple pencil because the graphite contained in pencils is conductive and can cause short circuits and potentially fires.

***

Postwoman Galina Yermolova uses a monster truck made by a friend to get supplies to her isolated Siberian town.

***

Hairdresser Alberto Olmedo in Madrid, Spain was disappointed with normal scissors and inspired by medieval barbers, cuts hair with a samurai sword, a blow torch, and metal claws.

***

Lying flat on your back with arms and legs spread is your best bet for surviving a falling elevator.

***

Almon Strowger invented the automatic telephone exchange, which eliminated the need for operators, after he learned he was losing business because the wife of his competitor was redirecting calls asking for Strowger to her husband.

***

The Twinkie was invented by James Dewar who worked as a baker for Continental Baking Company. He repurposed several machines used to make cream-filled strawberry shortcake that were sitting idle while strawberries were out of season. The original recipe used a banana cream.

***

In space, the zero gravity causes all your bodily fluids to move towards your head. This can often cause a headache which can best be alleviated by urinating.

***

People who laugh more are better able to tolerate pain - both physical and emotional. Additionally, laughing together with others is more effective than laughing alone.

***

The world's most expensive bottle of water, Acqua Di Cristallo Tributo a Modigliani, priced at $51,500, thanks to its hand-made 24-carat gold bottle.

***

Northern Collared Lemmings build underground 'toilets' and always defecate there so that their ultraviolet feces doesn't attract birds of prey.

***

The Romans weaved fire-retardant asbestos fibers into their napkins and tablecloths. They then cleaned them by throwing them into a hot fire and this made them even whiter than before.

***

A twelve-year-old from Memphis named Jackson Oswalt built a fusion nuclear reactor in his playroom and became the youngest person to do so, replacing the previous record which was 14 years of age.

***

New research shows ants manage large infrastructure projects without wasting any energy on coordination or communication between ants. Each ant works alone and solves problems by themselves.

***

Echolalia is the urge to imitate what someone has said and in the exact same voice.

***

A recent UK survey found that more than half of couples do not consummate the marriage on their wedding night, primarily because the groom is too drunk.

***

The 'XXX' which is often used to indicate "poison" originated from moonshiners. The X's indicated their alcohol had been run through the still 3 times and was now pure and strong.

***

There is a well-documented Koro (or genital retraction syndrome) epidemic that occurred in Singapore in late 1967. Men believed they were going to die from their penis shrinking after eating bad pork.

***

The first online e-commerce transaction ever was Stanford students buying marijuana from MIT students.

***

Researchers believe the tale of Jack And The Beanstalk is over 5,000 years old and was originally known as The Boy Who Stole Ogre's Treasure.

***

There's a genus of fly called Pieza which has cleverly named species like Pieza pie, Pieza rhea, Pieza kake, and finally the Pieza deresistans.

***

An actor named Joe Maggard lied to the media about portraying Ronald McDonald for 12 years. A 2014 documentary titled Ronald perpetuates his lie as he tells about his life after supposedly being Ronald McDonald.

***

The CIA spent $20 million in an attempt to use cats to spy on the Kremlin and Soviet embassies. The mission was called Acoustic Kitty and involved implanting a microphone in a cat's ears and a radio transmitter near its skull.

***

Britain's oldest turkey is ironically named 'Dinner'. He is over 16 years old and lives as a pet on Stonebridge Farm in Nottingham.

***

The USPS has ~1,700 employees in Utah whose sole job is to read illegible addresses which the machine can't read. They process 5 million pieces of mail daily with some employees averaging 1,600 addresses an hour.

***

YouTube is the second largest "search engine", right after Google. It's bigger than Bing, Yahoo!, and Ask combined.

***

A recent study found that a messy kitchen causes people to eat more. The chaotic environment causes people to feel out of control and to subsequently eat more.

***

Up until 2007, the Soviets had a three-barrel (2 shotgun and one rifled) space pistol in their Soyuz capsule in case they were stranded in the Siberian wilderness upon re-entry. The TP-82 also had a detachable butt-stock that was a machete.

***

Canada consumes the most doughnuts and has the most doughnut shops per capita of any country in the world.

***

A recent study found 1/3rd of the fish sold in restaurants and grocery stores in the US is mislabeled and misrepresented.

***

The origin of being "in the limelight" comes from the days before electricity when theatres had to produce spotlight by directing a flame at calcium oxide or quicklime. This was known as a limelight.

***

When a crocodile loses a tooth, it is quickly replaced by a new tooth. They can go through 8000 teeth over a lifetime.

***

Beginning in high school, Luca Iaconi-Stewart spent 9 years and ~10,000 hours building a 1/60-scale model of a Boeing 777 out of manila folders.

***

A recent study done by Stanford researchers found a positive correlation between the use of profanity and honesty. The individuals who use profanity tend to be more honest.

***

Frankie Muniz suffers from long-term memory loss and doesn't even remember starring in the TV show Malcolm in the Middle.

***

The first Wimbledon tennis tournament held on July 9, 1877 was only for amateurs. It was hosted by the All England Croquet and Lawn Tennis Club.

***

Wedding rings are placed on the left ring finger because in ancient times people used to believe it was the only finger where a vein connected straight to the heart.

***

Gary Hart was a Presidential candidate in 1988 and an alleged womanizer. He invited the media to follow him around to prove his innocence. The media accepted his invite and he was caught having an affair two weeks later.

***

There are two main thoroughfares in the capital of Kosovo named after former US Presidents. One is named George Bush Boulevard and parallel to it is Bill Clinton Boulevard.

***

The Nintendo Entertainment System became so popular in the 1990's that Nintendo Corp. had to campaign against calling all video game consoles a 'nintendo' in order to prevent their trademark from becoming generic.

***

Scientists have developed a micro particle filled with oxygen that can be injected into the blood flow, allowing us to live without breathing.

***

In 2016, the Swedish Tourist Association created a service where you could call a number and speak to a random Swede. It received nearly 200,000 calls over 79 days with an average duration of just under 3 min.

***

There's a small town in Washington named 'George'. Each year, George, Washington celebrates July 4th by baking a massive cherry pie.

***

Billy Ray Harris is a beggar who was accidentally given a $4000 engagement ring by a passing woman when she dropped it into his cup. He held on to it and two days later the woman came back for her ring and he gave it to her. In thanks, she set up a fund that raised over $185000 for him.

***

Xian'er, which translates to Worthy Stupid Robot Monk, is a robotic monk at China's Longquan Buddhist temple which is designed to interact with tourists.

***

The Orca or Killer Whale is one of the few natural predators of a moose. They prey on moose swimming between islands on the Northwest coast of North America.

***

A Japanese chef prepared an egg noodle measuring 602 feet, 9 inches long to break the Guinness World Record.

***

There are elevators in Singapore which are equipped with Urine Detection Devices. If triggered, the elevator will stop and the police are called.

***

Researchers have historically avoided using female animals in medical studies so they don't need to account for influences of their hormonal cycles. This can result in medications that don't work as well on females as males.

***

A study of 3,000 Brits found that 7:26 PM on Saturday is the happiest time of the week when they can finally unwind. The lowest time was during the commute at 7:29 AM Monday.

***

Koumpounophobia is the fear of buttons. Steve Jobs was afraid of buttons and therefore wore turtlenecks and a number of Apple's product designs are button-less because of his aversion.

***

Medieval dentists had many of the same skill-sets as modern dentists. They could fill cavities, treat facial fractures, spot oral cancer, and whiten teeth. Additionally, they could make dentures out of cow bone and human teeth.

***

A sea turtle patrol on Hilton Island in South Carolina has recently turned up a rare double-headed (bicephalic) hatchling, which they named Squirt and Crush.

***

The masked birch caterpillar uses anal drumming to find friends to build a communal silken shelter.

***

A study of 2500 men found having an orgasm at least 3 times a week cuts in half the likelihood of coronary heart disease.

***

The origin of Walt Disney's last name is the anglicized word D'Isigny meaning "from Isigny". Relatives in France created a cheese company and they've created collaborations making Mickey Mouse themed cheese.

***

Coke has 20 different brands that generate more than a billion dollars in sales globally.

***

There is a small hopping insect known as Issus Coleoptratus which has toothed gears in its joints to precisely synchronize its legs while jumping. They are the only mechanical gears which have been found in nature.

***

A family taking a walk on a beach in Wales found a message in a bottle thrown into the ocean by a German couple 1,624 miles away and nearly four years earlier.

***

In a study done by British "sensory branding company" Condiment Junkie, 96% of people can tell the difference between cold and hot water being poured.

***

Two men in Indiana were wrongfully convicted of armed robbery in 1996. The lead detective that set them up eventually resigned in 2001, but the records detailing his resignation went missing ever since. 20 years later they were found and the inmates were finally exonerated and received a nearly $5 million settlement.

***

The world's "biggest family" belongs to a man with 39 wives, 94 children and 33 grandchildren. They live together in a 100-room mansion in India.

***

Stone Man Syndrome is an extremely rare condition whereby any small damage to tissue is regrown into bone.

***

The human brain is full of multi-dimensional geometrical structures operating in as many as 11 dimensions.

***

During WWII, British scientist R.V Jones figured out how the German's 'Wotan' radar system worked by assuming it used a single beam since Wotan was a Germanic god with a single eye.

***

Sand wasps fly backwards out of their nest in order to be able to find their way back to it.

***

After undergoing IVF treatment, a 74-year-old woman has given birth to twin girls in an Indian nursing home.

***

There are five major American cities with water so pure it doesn't require filtration: Boston, San Francisco, Seattle, Portland, and NYC.

***

There are hundreds of species of spiders that disguise themselves as ants by pretending their two front legs are antennae in order to hide from predators and hunt their prey.

***

Research done by the University of York has shown that dogs actually like the silly, high-pitched voice their owners use to talk to them. "Dog-speak" is important in building a bond between a dog and their owner say scientists.

***

When faced with a life-or-death decision about choosing to move to a new hive, Honey Bees collectively fact-find and then decide democratically.

***

A colleague of Albert Einstein, Kurt Gödel, who was a brilliant mathematician and often cited as the greatest logician since Aristotle, survived on a diet of baby food, butter, and laxatives.

***

UK researcher FitRated found that the free weights at the gym have 362 times more bacteria than a toilet seat and treadmills had 74 times more bacteria than a bathroom faucet.

***

In Shanghai, you can get Coffee mellow, which is a coffee served with a cloud of cotton candy. The coffee vapor rises and dissolves the cotton candy which rains sugar into the cup.

***

The language of the Ewok's in Star Wars is Tibetan with some pieces of Nepalese.

***

A woman from Stockholm, Sweden, attempted to smuggle 75 live snakes onto an airplane by placing them in her bra. She also had six lizards under her shorts.

***

The webcam was invented because 3 faculty members at Cambridge University wanted to see the coffee levels in the break room so they didn't waste a trip there to find an empty pot.

***

Bruno's casque-headed frog (Aparasphenodon brunoi) is so venomous that 1 gram of its venom could kill 80 people or 300,000 mice.

***

Delia Bacon wrote a 682-page book backed by minimal research trying to prove that Shakespeare didn't write his plays. She showed up night after night at the church where Francis Bacon was buried trying to get access to his tomb where she thought he hid proof of his authorship.

***

The only place that can legally sell hard alcohol in Virginia are ABC Stores. They are owned and operated by the state, employing ~4000 employees in ~370 stores, generating hundreds of millions in revenue for VA.

***

A dead gecko can stick to a surface for up to 30 minutes after its death. Research has shown their sticking force is passive and just as effective dead or alive.

***

An Australian man and his two daughters found a gold nugget weighing 624 grams (worth ~$35,000) while walking their dog.

***

Over 50% of pilots surveyed in the U.K., Norway, and Sweden admitted to have fallen asleep while flying a passenger plane. A third of them stated that when they woke up, they discovered that their co-pilots had also fallen asleep.

***

The blue-banded bee (Amegilla murrayensis) head-bangs flowers 350x a second in order to obtain pollen.

***

William G. Thilly, the inventor of Apple Jacks cereal, is now a professor of biological engineering at MIT and invented the cereal while he was a summer intern.

***

Rick Rescorla saved all but 6 of his 2700 employees during the 9/11 attacks by directing people down the stairs using a bullhorn and encouraging them by singing Cornish songs.

***

The British have a one in 300 chance of being related to a complete stranger they meet in their homeland.

***

In 1951, Walt Disney hired a maid named Thelma Howard. He gifted her shares of Disney stock each Christmas. When she died in 1994, she had 192,000 shares worth $9 million. She left the majority to her foundation supporting disadvantaged kids.

***

Researchers have developed an efficient and eco-friendly catalytic reactor that can convert the common air pollutant CO_2 into high concentrations of pure formic acid, which can be used as a liquid fuel.

***

In 1844, there was a case of hysteria in a French convent of nuns. One started meowing and after a week all the nuns were meowing harmoniously in the afternoons. It didn't stop until neighbors called soldiers.

***

A study found store-bought tomatoes taste bland because they are missing the gene (TomLoxC) which gives them their flavor. 93% of the current, domesticated varieties sold in stores are missing the gene.

***

The St. Louis City Museum has the largest graphite pencil in the world. It is 76 feet long and weighs 18,000 pounds.

***

The modern high jump technique was created by Dick Fosbury and was dubbed the Fosbury Flop. Prior to the 1968 Olympics, the landing area was sand or low mats so jumpers needed to land on their feet or otherwise very carefully.

***

Contagious yawning, a common form of echophenomena (the automatic imitation of another's words or actions), is a real thing but scientists don't fully understand which part of the brain controls it.

***

Han Van Meegeren was a Dutch painter and forger who became a national hero after WWII when it was revealed he sold fake paintings to Nazi leaders. After initially being accused of treason for selling Dutch cultural artifacts to the Nazi's, he pleaded guilty to forgery and painted at his trial to prove he could replicate the famous Vermeer artwork.

***

The Japanese word kamikaze, meaning 'divine winds', originally referred to the typhoon that nearly destroyed the entire Mongol fleet, effectively preventing the second and last Mongol invasion of Japan, in 1281.

***

In 2017, a woman who received a uterus transplant from a deceased donor was able to give birth to a healthy baby.

***

Komodo dragons are protected from attack by an intricate chainmail armor made of tiny bones beneath their skin that develop in adulthood.

***

Latin had ~800 "dirty" words compared to the ~20 we have in modern English.

***

Zootopia is the only movie without a human character to make over $1 billion in worldwide movie theater ticket sales.

***

The aptly named Goliath frog, which can weigh over 6 lb., use their muscles to lift rocks over half their bodyweight to build small nursery ponds for their spawn.

***

Since the streets are often congested, Dubai has equipped some of their firefighters with a jet ski and water "jetpack" combo called the Dolphin which can be deployed from the many waterways.

***

The Matrix production designer Simon Whiteley confirmed that the green falling code in the Matrix is loads of sushi recipes.

***

NASA cleverly chose the name Juno for its Jupiter mission. Jupiter's moons are named after the god's many mistresses. The Juno space probe sent to monitor Jupiter is named after his wife.

***

Former Uruguayan President José Mujica spent over 12 years in prison. He escaped and was recaptured twice, and then confined to the bottom of an old, emptied horse-watering trough for more than two years.

***

Gorillas sing happy songs while they eat. They don't sing the same song every time, and they sing louder while eating their favorite food.

***

In the 1820's, a Cherokee named Sequoyah invented a writing system with 85 characters that was considered by many superior to the English alphabet. It could be learned in a few weeks and within a couple years majority of the Cherokees could read and write.

***

The movie The Godfather does not contain the words 'mafia' or 'la cosa nostra' because of a deal struck between the producer and the mafia.

***

"Häagen-Dazs" is a completely made up name by its Polish Jewish founders to try and sound Danish. The umlaut doesn't exist in Danish nor does the "zs" letter combination.

***

A professor at Texas A&M Galveston failed his entire class and quit, because he thought that all of his students were disruptive or dishonest and therefore didn't deserve to pass the course. This was his worst in his 20 years of teaching.

***

The record for the longest pregnancy is held by Beulah Hunter who in 1945 was pregnant for a year and 10 days, nearly 100 days longer than the average pregnancy.

***

Sarah the cheetah holds the planet-wide record for the fastest 100-meter dash, finishing in 5.95 seconds at a speed of 61 mph.

***

MIT engineers have created a robotic, snake-like thread that can navigate through narrow blood vessels in the brain, promising treatment for strokes and other blockages.

***

The Western Winter Wren can sing 36 notes per second, more than double the 16 notes that the Eastern version can sing.

***

In the early 20th century, the Prussian rulers prohibited the Danes in the area from displaying the Danish flag. In protest, they bred and displayed Husum Red Pied pigs that's coloring resembled the flag of Denmark.

***

A Welsh community built 2,044 sandcastles on the Whitmore Bay beach to break a Guinness World Record.

***

Anthropologists can partly determine the ancestral routes of different people and how those ancestors got to where their descendants now live by examining earwax.

***

An international team of scientists and Google engineers have discovered that the Rubik's cube puzzle can always be solved in 20 moves or less.

***

The ancient murrelet is the only bird known to migrate across the entire North Pacific. Many migrate 5,000 miles from Canada to winter near Japan and China, even though the climate is nearly identical.

***

Japan proposed an amendment to the Treaty of Versailles to abolish all racial discrimination. The US and Australia were the only opposition to it and so it was not included. As a compromise, Japan received a number of Pacific islands instead.

***

The world's largest serving of fried chicken totaling 3,675 pounds was prepared by 18 vendors at a food festival in Japan for a new Guinness World Record.

***

The ancient Greek word for a person aroused by garlic is Physiggoomai.

***

Before 1996, travelers were not required to present any form of ID before boarding a plane and a large secondary market for airline tickets existed. It was finally implemented as a knee-jerk response to the TWA flight 800 mystery.

***

In 1969, Astronauts embarking on the Apollo 11 space mission were unable to get life insurance so instead they sent their families autographed & postmarked envelopes.

***

In 1964, a kangaroo got stuck in the elevator at Television Centre during the launch of BBC2.

***

During the Great Depression, Arkansas's treasurer reported a balance of $4.62 for the entire general revenue fund of the state.

***

Blue eyes don't have blue pigment but are instead blue because they scatter light so that only blue light reflects out, similar to the sky and water.

***

The world's most expensive perfume is Clive Christian No. 1 Passant Guardant. It costs $143,000 for 30ml and comes in a flask studded with 2,000 diamonds.

***

A study found you are more likely to have nightmares if you sleep on your left side instead of your right.

***

In 1294, Pope Celestine V was elected after a two-year impasse. He was a monk and hermit before being elected and passed an edict allowing Popes to abdicate, which he did a week after issuing the decree and ~5 months as Pope.

***

The first television broadcast took place in 1925. It was a done with a grey scale image in a 30-line vertically scanned format, at five pictures per second using a ventriloquist's dummy nicknamed "Stooky Bill".

***

There is a DIY Netflix Project which creates a pair of socks that will pause what you're watching if you fall asleep while watching.

***

Alcatraz's reputation as a tough place to be imprisoned was a Hollywood myth. Many inmates requested a transfer there because it had good food, hot showers, and a one man per cell policy.

***

Human saliva contains a painkiller called Opiophin that is roughly 6 times more powerful than morphine.

***

In order to receive a passport, Dutch immigrants must watch a two-hour video which includes beach nudity as a way of making them aware of the Netherlands's liberal values.

***

In the remote Pilbara region of Australia, an aboriginal community built a train to carry their children to school. The train cars are made from metal barrels, and the locomotive is a tractor.

***

An upside-down pineapple in your grocery cart, or as a bumper sticker, or an upside-down door knocker indicates the person is into swinging.

***

The inventor of the USB standard Ajay Bhatt intended for it to be reversible but the idea was abandoned due to additional cost. Despite it becoming the standard, he regrets the decision.

***

Some slaughterhouses use a 'Judas goat'. It's a trained goat that will calmly lead livestock to their slaughter while its own life is spared.

***

Tigers are orange in color because their main prey, deer, see them as green. Deer are only capable of seeing blue and green light, which makes them color-blind to red.

***

There's a town in Alaska named Chicken. The citizens wanted to name it Ptarmigan after a popular local bird but they couldn't agree on the spelling so they went with chicken instead.

***

In 1936, Vladimir Lukyanov built a water (integrator) computer. It was the world's first computer for solving (partial) differential equations for Russia.

***

Mark Zuckerberg created an AI assistant for his home named Jarvis, after the butler in Iron Man, that is voiced by Morgan Freeman.

***

Michael Jackson's hair caught on fire at the exact middle of his life, down to the day. He lived 18,565 days and on day 9,283 (Jan 27, 1984) his hair caught on fire during a Pepsi commercial shoot.

***

Avocados nearly went extinct 13,000 years ago after large animals like the mammoth and giant ground sloth went extinct. With no means of dispersing the seeds, it was left to early farmers to cultivate the species.

***

The anthropologist Grover Krantz, who was infamous for believing in Bigfoot's existence, donated his body to the Smithsonian on the condition his dogs were kept close to him. The museum honored his request.

***

Viking's accidentally made a rudimentary form of steel when they tried to fuse the spirit of an animal or ancestor into a weapon. They would crush bones and fuse it into iron when forging weapons.

***

In 2012, Choi Gap-bok escaped from prison by squeezing his body through a 5.9" tall and 17.7" wide food slot when the guards were sleeping. He is a yoga practitioner and applied skin ointment to his body in order to slip out.

***

In 2018, Snoop Dogg set the world record for the largest paradise cocktail with a ~132-gallon gin and juice at the BottleRock Napa Valley music festival. It contained 180 bottles of gin, 154 bottles of apricot brandy, and just 38 jugs of orange juice.

***

The Washington Monument is capped with a 9", 100-ounce aluminum pyramid. Aluminum was a precious metal in 1884 and the pyramid was displayed at Tiffany's jewelry store in New York before it was placed at the top.

***

In 1912, Jim Thorpe, an American Indian, won two Olympic gold medals with a mismatched pair of shoes taken from the garbage.

***

German WW2 prisoners of war were treated so well in Canadian prisons that many didn't want to leave the country when released. Thousands of PoW's stayed in Canada or came back years later.

***

The Toddlers' Truce was a piece of British TV scheduling policy in the 1940's that required transmissions to stop between 6pm and 7pm. Children's programming ended at 6, which allowed young children to be put to bed before the evening programming at 7.

***

The hairy frogfish (Antennarius striatus) uses a vacuum in its mouth to suck in prey that is as large as it is in just 1/6000th of a second. Despite having only 5mm palatal teeth, it has the fastest 'bite' in the animal kingdom.

***

An endangered parrot in New Zealand was only mating with people's heads, so they made as 'ejaculation helmet' for people to wear which would collect the bird's rare semen.

***

According to a study with data sourced from phone apps, women on average tend to sleep a half hour longer than men, with women ages 25 and under getting the most sleep out of all.

***

The world's largest model train set in Germany beat its own Guinness World Record by adding a large new section based on Monaco. It previously measured 39,370 feet of track and has now expanded to 51,558 feet, 4.78 inches of track.

***

A Louisiana school principal resigned by text after being arrested standing in the middle of a street for public intoxication. He was found outside a strip club where he refused to pay his bill, all while he was on a school trip to Washington D.C.

***

Up until 1858, all British Passports were written in French. The International Civil Aviation Organization standard today recommends that, where the language of the issuing state is English, French or Spanish, they should supplement with one of the other languages.

***

When Steve Madden, founder and CEO of the footwear company, was convicted of fraud and forced to resign, he created a new consultant position for himself that paid him $700k a year while in prison.

***

China is the world's largest mobile games market, accounting for over 25 per cent of global revenue. Domestic games revenue in China is expected to reach a staggering total of $42 billion by 2022.

***

In 1955, the Zion Meat Company held a beauty pageant during their national hot dog week and declared Geene Courtney the Sausage Queen.

***

During the Great Depression, a banker convinced families in Quincy, Florida to buy Coca-Cola shares for $19 apiece. The town later became the single richest per capita in the USA with 67 millionaires.

***

IBM launched the 305 RAMAC, the first computer with a hard disk drive (HDD) in September 1956. The HDD weighed over a ton and stored 5MB of data.

***

In Germany, those who urinate in the streets are known as wildpinklers, meaning "free pee-ers".

***

Your tooth enamel is harder than a lobster's shell or a rhino's horn. It's even harder than steel. It's made of mineralized calcium phosphate, which is the hardest substance a living being can produce.

***

The Colombian river Cano Cristales is commonly called the River of Five Colors or Liquid Rainbow because of its striking colors.

***

A study found that each year arthropods (like millipedes, spiders and ants) eat over 2,100 pounds of junk food discarded in New York City's Broadway/West St. corridor in Manhattan. That's the equivalent of 60,000 hot dogs.

***

You receive a higher dose of radiation living next to a coal plant than you do a nuclear plant. This is due to the fly ash emitted by the power plant which is 100x more radiation than a similar nuclear plants waste.

***

There's a type of honey called mad honey which causes hallucinations. Honey hunters in Nepal make the dangerous vertical climb to harvest it because it sells for up to $80 a pound.

***

Nematode's (also known as the roundworm) sperm does not swim but crawls using its cytoskeleton instead.

***

A 2015 research study on the efficiency of mosquito repellents found that Victoria's Secret's Bombshell perfume actually repelled mosquito's better than nearly all the other non-DEET products.

***

There were Shingon Monks who successfully mummified themselves alive via a practice called Sokushinbutsu, meaning "a Buddha in this very body". Only 24 such mummifications have been discovered to date.

***

Flatworms have male and female sets of genitalia, and if they can't find a flatworm to mate with, they will inseminate themselves by stabbing their head with their needle-like copulatory organ, a practice known as selfing.

***

Bob Graham, the former Governor and Senator of Florida, worked 408 'work days' starting in 1974 as part of his political campaigns. He performed various jobs in Florida for a full eight-hour workday, including working as a barber, "pooper scooper", bellhop, tomato picker, etc.

***

In 2010, the Colombian army produced a song called 'Better Days' with Morse code embedded in the chorus and aired it in rebel-controlled territory to lift the morale of hostages. The message said "19 people rescued. You are next. Don't lose hope."

***

One of the largest and oldest organisms on Earth, the 'Trembling Giant', is slowly dying to mule deer. The 106-acre pando quaking aspen colony in Utah, which is nearly 80,000 years old, is being thinned by the deer eating its new stems. The mule deer are thriving as they currently have no natural predators.

***

A recent study on plastic pollution found the average person consumes 50,000 particles of microplastic a year and breathes in roughly the same amount.

***

The world's longest water slide was unveiled in Malaysia and is a 1-kilometer-long chute that starts on a hilltop. It is three times longer than the previous record-holding slide in Germany.

***

Americans are over 20 times more likely to be killed by a cow than by a shark, bear, or alligator.

***

The four construction bay doors on NASA's Vehicle Assembly Building (or VAB) are the world's largest doors. At 456 feet high, they are taller than the Statue of Liberty.

***

There's a 2001 cult film called Jesus Christ Vampire Hunter. The plot has a modern-day Jesus struggling to protect the lesbians of Ottowa, Ontario from vampire with the help of Mexican wrestler El Santo.

***

A recent study found children are 39% more likely to buy a particular brand of automobile if their parents bought that brand.

***

A professional eater downed 50 slices of pumpkin pie in 10 minutes to win a New York state contest and set a new record for the event.

***

Muhammad Ali's star on the Hollywood walk of fame is not on the sidewalk. It is on the wall of Kodak/Dolby theater because of his request that the name of Muhammad not be walked on.

***

In 2004, after a particularly bad locust plague in Australia, two local agricultural officers created a more palatable name and cook book with 20 "sky prawn" recipes titled Cooking With Sky Prawns.

***

India set a new world record planting over 66 million trees in 12 hours. The Madhya Pradesh state used 1.5 million volunteers to plant the saplings along the Narmada river.

***

The puffin's beak is specialized to hold lots of fish. They can carry roughly 5-20 fish back to their nest at a time. Astonishingly, a puffin in Britain once carried 62 fish in his beak!

***

In 2016, the United Kingdom spent over $96000 to create a national sperm bank and ended up with 7 donors before shutting down 2 years later.

***

Dan Aykroyd has both Tourette's and Asperger's and was born with webbed toes and two different colored eyes. He also has an obsession with police and ghosts, which is how the idea of Ghostbusters came to be.

***

In 2019, the world's first human-monkey hybrid was created in China. Scientists injected human stem cells into the monkey embryo to create the animal-human hybrid. The experiment was stopped before the birth.

***

In 2015, a teenager named Bud Weisser was arrested for trespassing in a secure area at the Budweiser Brewery located in St. Louis.

***

The oceans are filled with giant tubular organisms that grow to the size of sperm whales. They are known as Pyrosomes or unicorns of the sea and can be nearly 60 ft in length.

***

A team of 20 sherpas cleaned up and removed 11 metric tons of garbage and four dead bodies from Mt. Everest in April and May of 2019.

***

Oceanographers and engineers in California have created 'snotbots', which are drones that collect spray from whales' blowholes.

***

Facebook created two AI chatbots named Alice and Bob but shut them down when they stopped communicating in English because it wasn't as efficient as the language they developed themselves.

***

An ancient shark fossil that looks a lot like an eel was found in Morocco. The fossil belongs to the ancient shark genus Phoebodus which lived 360 million years ago.

***

Researchers found African cotton leafworm moths remember the kind of plant where they mated for the very first time and will return to that plant species to mate again.

***

In 2012, a Cleveland woman arrested for a traffic violation was ordered to share her crime by holding a sign for 2 days that read 'only an idiot would drive on the sidewalk to avoid a school bus.'

***

The first cell phone was the Motorola DynaTAC 8000X aka 'The Brick'. It was designed by Rudy Krolopp in April of 1984 and sold in the United States for just under $4,000. It weighed two pounds.

***

The French phrase *rire dans sa barbe* translates 'to laugh in one's beard' meaning to laugh quietly about a past event.

***

The world's oldest astronomical clock still operating is the 'Prague Orloj' in Prague. The clock was first installed in 1410, making it the third-oldest astronomical clock in the world.

***

Orthosomnia is a new disorder where people are so obsessed with the quality of their sleep that they lose sleep because of it.

***

The Ainu people of Japan carved libation sticks, which were originally thought to be mustache lifters to keep the man's hair out of the way while drinking sake, but their actual purpose is to help send prayers to the gods during religious ceremonies.

***

The Antikythera Mechanism is the oldest known "computer" in the world. It was used to predict astronomical positions and eclipses for calendrical and astrological purposes and was developed in the second or first century BC.

***

A jelly bean takes anywhere from 7 to 21 days to make. It starts with liquid sugar and flavors being heated and mixed with starch and glucose. More sugar is added to give it a hard shell plus hot syrup and wax are applied to give it a shiny finish - all over the course of many days of processing.

***

Hoia Baciu is known as one of the world's most haunted forests and is dubbed the 'Bermuda Triangle of Romania' as many people have gone missing in the woods. Visitors often report feeling like they are being watched or suffer sudden anxiety.

***

A cat named Grace helped save her owners from carbon monoxide poisoning by repeatedly banging on their old 120-year-old home's bedroom door to wake them.

***

Studies show that about 85% of people only breathe out of one of their nostrils at a time. There is a nasal cycle which rotates between the two every ~4 hours.

***

Dogs can tell time by smell. They can smell different times of the day and how long their owner has been gone by how much their smell has dissipated since they left.

***

Paleolithic humans stored the bone marrow in legs of deer for delayed consumption (up to 9 weeks later) as early as 400,000 years ago.

***

Researchers found the Puff adder uses both visual and chemical camouflage (minimizing their scent) to hide from predators and ambush prey.

***

The Maricopa County Animal Care and Control center offers a 'Calming Companions' program where the public can visit their shelters to play with and keep the animals calm during 4th of July fireworks.

***

Since 1979, Jadav Payeng aka The Forest Man of India has been planting trees every day on the island of Majuli and Jorhat. In that time, he has built a forest reserve covering 1,360 acres and now that place has its own ecosystem.

***

Nintendo started as a playing card company in 1889 and over the years has operated a taxi company called "Daiya" as well as an hourly 'love hotel'.

***

Mario Puzo, the author of The Godfather books who helped adapt them to film, had no formal training and had never written a screenplay before. After winning two Oscars for the first two movies, he decided to buy a book to help him learn to how to screenwrite.

***

People with very sensitive noses are capable of smelling when it's about to rain due to atmospheric chemicals reacting and creating ozone, which has a pungent, sweet smell. The thunderstorm's downdrafts carry it from higher altitudes to nose level.

***

Greenland extends farther East of, West of, South of, and North of Iceland.

***

WRBH in New Orleans is a radio station for the blind. Each day volunteers read the local newspaper on the air, along with best-sellers, grocery ads, stories for kids, mysteries, the Wall Street Journal, young adult novels and more.

***

Google offers employees free condoms in their campus health center that come in blue, red, green, and yellow and have their trademark 'I'm Feeling Lucky!' printed on them.

***

Researchers taught rats how to gamble and they learned how to play it safe and maximize their 'winnings'. However, when they introduced flashing lights and sounds, they changed their behavior and went for the high-risk, high-reward option.

***

Dashrath Manjhi, known as 'Mountain Man', carved a path 360 ft long, 30 ft wide and 25 ft deep through a hill using only a hammer and chisel in India. It took him 22 years but it shortened the journey from 34 miles down to 9.

***

The Luftwaffe planted rescue buoys (Rettungsboje) in the English Channel for downed pilots to survive in. They contained food, alcohol, clothing and games.

***

In a group of clownfish, there is only one female who is at the top of a strict hierarchy. Only two clownfish in a group reproduce through external fertilization. They are also hermaphrodites, so when the female dies, the largest and most dominant male becomes a female.

***

The 1933 Double Eagle was a $20 coin made of gold that sold at auction for more than $7.5 million. More than 445,500 coins were minted, but they were never officially circulated and almost all of them were melted down.

***

According to Indeed.com, jobs available for 'Ninjas' are up 2,505% since 2006. Jobs for "rock stars" or "rocksters" are up 810% and those for "Jedis" are up 67% in the same time period.

***

Castroville is a rural town in California that is nicknamed the 'Artichoke Capital of the World'. 99.9% of all artichokes worldwide are grown in California as they can grow them year-round there.

***

In an early alternative version of The Three Little Pigs by Andrew Lang, the pigs were named: Browny, Whitey, and Blacky. The antagonist was also a fox instead of a wolf.

***

Pistachios split themselves open when they are ripe in a process called dehiscence. This trait has been selected and specifically cultivated with different varieties having various rates of dehiscence consistency.

***

Bananas have a curved shape because they reach for the sunlight when they grow. This unique process is known as 'negative geotropism'.

***

In the early 1900's, Marshall Field's department store used professional scapegoat's or "fired men" who would take the blame and be fired to appease disgruntled customers.

***

The cockchafer, also known as a Maybug or doodlebug, is a European beetle which has three species: common, forest, and (the rarest) large cockchafer.

***

Since 2000, each member of the cast of Friends has been making $20 million per year thanks to syndication royalties. The studio WB is making nearly $1 billion each year.

***

Nearly 50% of all Brazilian models are from Brazil's Rio Grande do Sul state, while only 6% of the Brazil's total population lives there.

***

Michelangelo was the third sculptor to work on the famous statue of David. The piece of Carrara marble itself is of mediocre quality, stood out in the elements for ~25 years, and was known as the Duccio stone before Michelangelo sculpted it into a masterpiece.

***

An economist named Stefan Mandel and his investors won the lottery 14 times (the largest jackpot was $27 million) by calculating when the jackpot was worth more than the cost of buying every possible number combination for that lottery.

***

It takes over 500 years to produce just under an inch of topsoil, which is the most productive layer of soil. This soil is often derived from rock which has to be broken into smaller pieces through either physical or chemical weathering.

***

In some cultures and languages, the colors described in English as blue and green are colexified, or expressed using a single cover term.

***

A recent study found both humans and domestic dogs receive a dramatic increase of oxytocin, the bonding hormone, from the other when staring into each other's eyes.

***

Mothers are asked more questions per hour (23) than teachers (19) and doctors/nurses (18). They are asked the most around meal times (11), followed by while shopping (10), and then while reading a story (9).

***

Studies show that there are more bacteria cells (~39 trillion microbial cells) than human cells (~30 trillion cells) in our bodies. Even as many as 40 of our human genes are thought to be bacterial in origin.

***

After his son tragically died in an accident caused by a pothole, Dadarao Bilhore took it upon himself to fill potholes around Mumbai. Using sand, gravel, and cement collected from building sites, he has filled 600 potholes since 2015 and continues on.

***

The Pop-Tart was created after Post's pet food division created the technology for a non-refrigerated, semi-moist dog food called Gaines Burgers. Shortly after they launched Country Squares, but Kellogg later came out with their Pop-Tart and far better marketing.

***

'E' is the most common letter and appears in 11% of all English words. It is nearly 57 times more likely to appear in a word than the letter 'Q'.

***

Africa has roughly 18 sets of twins per 1000 births. It is the world's highest rate of twin-births among regions in the developing world. Igbo Ora Town in Nigeria averaged nearly 50 sets per 1000 births when studied in the 1970's.

***

In 2016, a British man crowdfunded a ten-hour film of paint drying in order to force the British Board of Film Classification to watch it. It was a protest against the BBFC requiring independent filmmakers pay £1000 per submission for their certificate.

***

Setenil de Las Bodegas is a place in Spain where 3,000 residents live, work, and play in a gorge beneath a huge, rocky outcropping - their homes are built into the rock underneath.

***

A startup company and the Mongolian government are teaming together to create a new postal code system. They assign each 3-meter square piece of land three-word postal code. There are enough words in the English dictionary to account for the 57 trillion 3-meter squares on Earth.

***

Archivist and researcher Thomas Hargrove, who works with the non-profit Murder Accountability Project (MAP), estimates that some 2,000 serial killers are at large in the United States.

***

The California sea hare, Aplysia californica, has a combination of defense mechanisms including the release of purple ink and opaline from glands. The ink acts as a smoke screen while the opaline confuses the predator and causes them to try to eat the ink cloud.

***

A woman named Marijuana Pepsi, who refused to change her name, earned her Ph.D. at age 46 after writing her thesis on "Black names in white classrooms: Teacher behaviors and student perceptions."

***

Maria Paraskeva of Cyprus fulfilled her childhood dream by wearing a lace veil that stretched 22,843 feet and 2.11 inches, or roughly 63.5 football fields which is a new Guinness world record.

***

In a recent study, researchers found that less than half of 168 modern cultures engaged in romantic kissing. They found societies with distinct social classes are more likely to be kissers than those with fewer or no social classes.

***

Kano Jigoro, the father of Judo, asked to be buried in his white belt to be remembered as a learner and not the black belt master that he was.

***

Archaeologists found a gruesome and shocking discovery in Peru, 100 dead guinea pigs that were sacrificed by the Incan people during the 16th century, adorned with earrings, necklaces, and some wrapped in small rugs.

***

The sale and production of Vodka was banned in Russia between 1914 and 1925. The Tsar issued the decree to assist with mobilization as Russia entered the First World War.

***

In 2016, Daisy Belle Ward, who is the oldest living leap year baby, celebrated her 25th birthday on her 100th year of life.

***

According to an Australian study, more people are diagnosed with serious heart conditions, including heart attacks, on Mondays than any other day of the week.

***

In 2013, Heineken attempted to feature Rev. CH Bulmer but inadvertently featured Hugh Price Hughes, a prominent Methodist, who spent his life helping alcoholics instead.

***

Article 247 of the Revised Penal Code in the Philippines allows one to 'legally' kill or physically injure their spouse or the person they are having sexual intercourse with if they catch them in the act of making love or right after. The penalty for the crime is destierro or banishment.

***

According to a recent study, watching high-quality television dramas can improve your emotional intelligence and enhance your ability to read other people's emotions.

***

Kermit the Frog originally started out on the show Sam and Friends in 1955 as a lizard-like creature made from an old turquoise coat belonging to Jim Henson's mom and a couple of ping pong balls for eyes.

***

Oliver "Porky" Bickar was so dedicated to April fools' pranks that he flew hundreds of tires into Mt. Edgecumbe, a dormant volcano near Sitka, Alaska, and set them on fire. He fooled both the locals and Coast Guard into thinking the volcano was active.

***

Since 1950, there have been 32 US nuclear weapon accidents, known as "Broken Arrows". As many as six have been lost and unaccounted for. The former USSR has lost 41 with an unknown amount of them recovered.

***

Israeli archaeologists and engineers are building what resembles a subway tunnel under a Palestinian neighborhood in Jerusalem to uncover an ancient stepped street to the foot of the former Temple Mount. The street is believed to have been commissioned by Pontius Pilate.

***

A new skate park in England will be called "The Skatey McSkateface" after a public vote on social media. The name amassed more votes than the second and third place names combined.

***

Dwayne Johnson is the first ever third-generation professional wrestler. Additionally, both his grandfather and father had ties to the Anoa'i family, a large family of wrestlers known as the Samoan Dynasty.

***

Wombats poop comes out in cubes. Researchers found that it takes this shape in the last 8 percent of their intestinal tract. This final section of the wombat's entrails has walls that apply pressure to their feces which forms it into cubes.

***

There's a 12-foot-tall replica of the Washington Monument concealed under a manhole on the grounds of the monument. It's used as a surveying tool, which is typically a simple metal rod, but because of its location this special version was installed.

***

When Milton Bradley Company introduced Twister in 1966 as a game of physical skill, it was denounced by their competitors as 'sex in a box'. It is one of the first games where human bodies are used as playing pieces.

***

The otherwise adorable duck-billed platypus (Ornithorhynchus anatinus) has a venomous spur on its hind legs. The spur is only on the males and is non-lethal to humans but can be extremely painful.

***

Pregnant women attract roughly twice as many mosquito bites as non-pregnant people. This is likely because they tend to exhale more carbon dioxide and have a higher body temperature than others.

***

Chock Full o' Nuts coffee was introduced in 1932; but it does not contain nuts. It's named for a chain of nut stores that the founder converted into coffee shops during the Great Depression.

***

Nearly 80% of all avocados sold in the world come from a single seed sourced in 1926. Rudolph Hass grafted the seedling with branches from a Fuerte avocado tree which he almost cut down.

***

Dysentery and chronic diarrhea were so prevalent during the American Civil War that there was an honor code among soldiers: you couldn't shoot a man while he was defecating.

***

People didn't always say 'hello' when they answered the phone. When the first regular phone service was established in 1878, Alexander Graham Bell suggested answering the phone with 'Ahoy!'

***

Insulin used to be combined with protamine, obtained from rainbow trout milt/semen, to prolong the effect.

***

Don Rickles, the voice of Mr. Potato Head, passed away before he was able to record any dialogue for Toy Story 4. Rather than replace him, Disney reviewed 25 years of material from the first three films, video games, and other media and were able to assemble enough dialogue to cover the entire film.

***

In 1953, a single PEEPS Marshmallow Chick took 27 hours to make and was created by hand with a pastry tube. Today, even with advances in technology it still takes about six minutes.

***

If they do not break on impact, both a glass and a steel ball of similar proportion to a rubber ball will bounce higher than the rubber ball.

***

Woody Guthrie wrote "This Land is Your Land" as a retort, after he got tired of hearing Kate Smith's "God Bless America" over and over again. He sarcastically named the song "God Blessed America For Me" before later changing the title.

***

The White Bellbird, found in the Guianas, Brazil and Venezuela, is known as the world's loudest bird. Their mating call sounds like a fire alarm and can reach up to 125 decibels.

***

Castoreum is a warm, carnal, and leather-like scent used in perfume. Now synthetically replicated, it originally came from the castor sac of the mature North American Beaver which was used in combination with urine to mark their territory.

***

Up until 1970, United Airlines had 'men only' flights featuring complimentary cigars, cocktails, and a full-course steak dinner in the exclusive company of other men.

***

According to a recent study, researchers found infants who get more hugs and physical contact have more developed brains.

***

In 1963, Winston Churchill was the first foreign national to receive honorary United States citizenship. He also received a passport-like document along with it which was not valid for travel.

***

Dr. William Stewart Halstead, the father of modern surgery, pioneered the use of anesthetics by experimentally injecting himself with cocaine. He eventually became addicted to cocaine and then morphine but somehow continued to modernize medical training.

***

In Toronto, Canada, a small company has developed vegan leather made from apple peels that are recycled from the juicing industry.

***

Alaska, Arizona, Indiana, Kentucky, Pennsylvania, Tennessee, Utah, and West Virginia all have official state firearms ranging from a single action revolver to a semi-automatic sniper rifle.

***

John Wayne was given his own island, which was named after him, off the coast of Panama to thank him for his support in returning control of the Panama Canal to Panama.

***

In a recent survey released by investment bank UBS, Munich was deemed the city with the highest risk of developing a housing bubble.

***

Wildlife trafficking, worth an estimated $10 billion a year, is thought to be the third most valuable illicit commerce after drugs and weapons. Birds are the most common contraband with anywhere from two million to five million wild birds smuggled yearly.

***

A man in South Florida won an auction with a winning bid of $13,000 for what he thought was a villa, but turned out to be a 12 in. x 100 ft. strip of land between two villas.

***

Guinness Book Of Records holds the record for being the book most often stolen from public libraries.

***

In the 1950's, the Canadian government developed the 'fruit machine' to identify gay men and remove them from their jobs in the civil service, military, and police.

***

Studies found redheaded females have up to a 25% higher pain threshold than the rest of us. Additionally, redheads can make their own supply of vitamin D and feel temperature changes more intensely, all thanks to their 'redhead gene' MC1R.

***

Honey hunters in Mozambique use special calls to recruit the services of birds known as honeyguides. The birds lead the humans to bees' nests and in return, they get the leftover beeswax.

***

Sport Utility Vehicles or SUVs, with their higher front-end profile, are at least twice as likely as cars to kill pedestrians; higher SUV sales have led to huge increase in pedestrian fatalities in the US during the past decade.

***

British artist Andy Goldsworthy arranges leaves, sticks, and stones, creating unbelievably magical land artworks. He creates transitory works of art that look almost as if they were formed naturally.

***

A study found that Botox injections to get rid of frown lines selectively impairs the ability to understand angry and sad sentences.

***

Greek Fire was an incendiary weapon developed by the Byzantines in the 7th century and was impervious to water. It was used on ship to ship combat, as well as in handheld tubes, operating similar to a flamethrower. Its precise chemical composition was a closely held secret that has been lost to history.

***

In 2008, Miyuki Hatoyama, who a year later became Japan's first lady, described traveling to Venus to witness an alien world in her book entitled "Very Strange Things I've Encountered."

***

In 1922, there were a series of riots in New York that lasted 8 days known as the Straw Hat Riot. They started because men were wearing straw hats past the date deemed socially acceptable - 15 September.

***

A mantis shrimp can swing its claw so fast that it boils the water around it and creates a flash of light.

***

The children's book The Very Hungry Caterpillar by Eric Carle was originally titled A Week with Willie Worm.

***

Researchers in France have developed a brain-controlled robotic suit that has allowed a paralyzed man to walk again. A tetraplegic man has spent two years moving a virtual avatar in a video game in order to train a decoding algorithm, which translates the signals into movements.

***

There aren't any true wild horses in the US any more. The Western US has a population of free-roaming mustangs that are descendants of domesticated colonial Spanish horses and therefore are technically feral and not wild.

***

The trap-jaw ant can bite with a force of over 300 times their own bodyweight. Their jaws snap shut at a record-setting speed of ~62 mph. By biting the ground, they can launch themselves in the air to avoid danger.

***

There's an old Finnish measurement unit called a poronkusema, which translates to "reindeer's piss". It describes the distance a reindeer can travel without having to stop to pee which is roughly 7 - 7.5km.

***

The Spanish national anthem, Marcha Real, has never officially had lyrics and has been played without any unofficial words since 1978.

***

Lewis Fry Richardson, considered the father of modern weather forecasting, derived many of the complex equations needed for weather prediction in the 1920's. However, the math was so difficult that to predict the weather for the next six hours took him six weeks to do the calculations.

***

Tardigrades, or "water bears", are semi-aquatic, microscopic animals typically 0.5 mm in length which can survive virtually anything like an active lava field or even the cold, dark vacuum of space.

***

Italians wear red underwear on New Year's Eve to bring them good luck. It is a tradition dating back to medieval times when the men would wear a red drape to protect the family jewels from witches.

***

The servant of Philon was an ancient Greek humanoid figure capable of automatically filling a wine cup when placed in its hand. It accomplished its task using a pneumatic system that was very advanced for its time.

***

Dead bodies can get goosebumps, those tiny little bumps on your arms, legs and neck when you get cold or have an eerie feeling. It is a result of rigor mortis which causes the contraction of the tiny muscles under the hair follicles and simulates goosebumps.

***

Poison dart frogs derive their toxicity from eating poisonous ants and termites in the wild. A captive-bred dart frog is essentially harmless, as its diet does not include any poisonous prey.

***

In a new study, researchers found that the human nose has roughly 400 scent receptors that can detect at least 1 trillion different odors, far more than the 10,000 previously thought.

***

The assassin bug wears the exoskeletons of its prey as removable armor. The armor is multi-purposed as it is used to intimidate larger predators and if another bug does try to attack, the bodies will peel off allowing it to escape.

***

In 1959, USPS delivery of mail by rocket took place for the first and last time. The USS Barbero, a submarine, fired an unarmed cruise missile carrying ~3,000 pieces of mail as its payload. It took 22 minutes to arrive to Naval Auxiliary Air State in Mayport.

***

The word muscle comes from the Latin musculus meaning little mouse. So-called because the shape and movement of some muscles (notably biceps) were thought to resemble mice under cloth.

***

In 2009, Liberia had to declare a state of emergency in 3 counties because of an African armyworm caterpillar invasion. Tens of millions of the larvae appeared and began eating through their green crops and contaminating the water supplies with their feces.

***

Patrick's Pub and Grill is a bar that's on the border of Georgia and Tennessee and split between the two states. The Georgia half is in a "dry county", meaning that any alcohol purchased at the bar on the Tennessee side cannot be brought to the Georgia side where the restrooms are.

***

One dung beetle can drag things that weigh ~1,141 times its own weight. That would be like an average human pulling six double-decker buses!

***

The Woozle Effect occurs when repetition of false statements that lack any evidence misleads people into thinking or believing there is evidence, resulting in nonfacts becoming urban legends.

***

Tate's Hell State Park is a 202,000-acre forest/swamp near Carrabelle, FL. Legend has it that it's named after a man that got lost in the wilderness. When he emerged, he told a passerby "My name is Cebe Tate, and I just came from Hell" before collapsing.

***

Camels can drink 30 gallons of water in just 13 minutes. The water is stored in the camel's bloodstream and not in its energy-rich fatty hump.

***

Seahorses don't have stomachs, just intestines for the absorption of nutrients from food. As such, food passes through their digestive system rapidly and they must eat almost constantly.

***

During the Secret War (1959-75) or 'Laotian Civil War', the United States flew more than half a million missions over the tiny southeast Asian nation and dropped more bombs than they did on Germany and Japan combined during World War 2.

***

The Swedish Peace and Arbitration Society created a sign dubbed the Singing Sailor to keep the Russian submarines out of their border. It displays an animated sailor in underwear thrusting his hips while broadcasting in Morse code: "This way if you are gay."

***

WIMPs (weakly interacting massive particles), WIMPzillas, and MACHOs (massive astrophysical compact halo object) are theoretical particles based on the theory of 'dark matter'.

***

Workers constructing Beijing's Forbidden City created an ice path to carry stones to the site. The path was lubricated with water as the sledges with the stones passed, reducing friction and letting them slide much easier before the water refroze.

***

Jaguars have such powerful jaws that they kill their prey by biting into the brain directly through the skull.

***

A recent study found limpet teeth, which they use to scrape food off rocks, are made from the strongest biological material in nature. The material the mollusk's teeth are made out of is about five times as strong as spider silk, the former title holder.

***

For over a century, locals in remote parts of India have been using trees to build root bridges, known locally as jing kieng jri. Taking 15 to 30 years to grow, they can span up to 250' above gorges and rivers and support up to 35 people at a time.

***

In 1978, rock band Aerosmith paid approximately $4200 to bail out every single fan that was arrested when cops invaded the crowd on a pot bust during one of their concerts.

***

Technically, France holds the record by having a dozen different time zones, more than the USA and Russia which each span 11 different time zones.

***

Robin Mathews won an Oscar for Best Achievement in Makeup and Hairstyling for the 2013 movie Dallas Buyers Club which had a makeup budget of only $250 for the entire 28 days of production.

***

Charles Darwin once made a list of the pros and cons for marriage, the pros included: 'constant companion and a friend in old age better than a dog anyhow.' The cons: 'less money for books' and 'terrible loss of time.'

***

A recent study found that pythons don't actually kill by suffocation, but rather by cutting off the circulation of blood resulting in a heart attack.

***

Leonardo Da Vinci once created a replica of a heart valve by pouring hot wax into an oxen's heart, making a mold of thin glass from the cast, and then pumping water mixed with seeds through it. He identified vortices which help close the heart valve after each beat.

***

In 2009, a four-year-old British boy and his father were searching a field in Hockley with his father's metal detector and discovered a 16th century golden pendant estimated to be worth $4 million.

***

The Rézfaszú bagoly, which translates to 'The Copper-Penis Owl', is the Hungarian equivalent of the boogeyman and used by parents to scare children into behaving properly.

***

Fireworks have been completely illegal in Florida since 1941, but are sold to people en masse via hundreds of stores across the state to anyone who signs a waiver saying they're for agricultural use to scare birds away from crops.

***

Since 1988, a dog breeder has been working on The Dire Wolf Project. The goal is creating a breed (American Alsatian) of loving companion dog that resembles a prehistoric dire wolf. They are enormous, scary, shaggy, and by all accounts, sweet.

***

In 1996, a man in Devon, England spent a year hooting at owls and logging their response only to find out his neighbor was unknowingly the 'owl' hooting back.

***

In early 2019, Hawaii tried to pass a law making the legal smoking age 100. They were also the first state to raise the legal age to 21 back in early 2017.

***

Nicholas Culpeper was a 17th-century physician who married a wealthy heiress, enabling him to provide his services free of charge. He also translated Latin medical texts into English and published them as self-help guides for use by the poor. He believed medicine was a public asset and not a commercial secret.

***

The Academy Awards originally handed out a golden statue called the Academy Award of Merit in 1929. However, the origination of how it became known as an Oscar is a mystery. One story claims that the then Academy librarian, Margaret Herrick, thought the statue resembled her uncle Oscar.

***

Every Rolls-Royce pinstripe is painted by Englishman Mark Court, a former village sign painter. It's the last manufacturing step and needs to be perfect as the paint instantly bonds with the car body and cannot be erased.

***

Researchers found that dogs have musical tastes. The Scottish SPCA and University of Glasgow monitored dogs' heart rates while playing different genres of music and found that they generally preferred reggae and soft rock.

***

Scientists believe the spruce and pine trees in the boreal forests of Siberia survive the -60 degrees Celsius temperatures by allowing their tree tissues to turn to glass as part of a process called 'hardening'.

***

Coffee was so important in Turkish culture that under 15th-century law, a woman had the freedom to divorce her husband if he did not provide her with enough coffee.

***

The black paint around the outside of your cars' windshield is called 'frit'. The frit band both hides the ugly sealant securing the windshield to your car and protects it from the sun's ultraviolet rays which can damage the adhesion.

***

Towards the end of World War 2, the Japanese began to use pine oil from pine tree roots to fuel their airplanes. Heating the roots and distilling the pine oil took 12 hours and only resulted in ~4 percent crude fuel.

***

The US federal government has an office in Denver called the National Eagle Repository that receives dead bald and golden eagles, which are then used by registered Native Americans tribes for religious and cultural ceremonies.

***

When the CEO of supermarket chain ALDI, Theo Albrecht, was kidnapped, he haggled down his ransom amount with his abductors and claimed the sum as a tax-deductible business expense in court after his release. He then became a recluse.

***

M&M's were first created commercially in 1941 by Forrest Mars, Sr. after witnessing soldiers eating chocolate pellets with a hard shell during the Spanish Civil War, which prevented the chocolate from melting in the warm weather.

***

Drooping ears is a trait for domesticated animals that very rarely occurs in the wild (elephants are an exception). Almost all species gain this trait when domesticated. A Russian experiment successfully domesticated foxes over 40 generations, and in that span their ears drooped.

***

Scientists studying the ocean floor in the Black Sea have found over 40 ships, some from as far back as the 9th century, that are so well preserved they can still see chisel and tool marks on the planks from the original builder.

***

Sgriob is a Gaelic word meaning "an itching of the lip, superstitiously supposed to precede a feast, a drink of whiskey, or a kiss from a favorite."

***

The iconic game Goldeneye 007 for the Nintendo 64 gaming system was created by a group of only 9 people, 8 of which had never worked on a video game before.

***

In early 2019, after McDonald's sued Irish fast food chain Supermac for trademark infringement, a judge ruled McDonald's Big Mac trademark was not valid in the EU because they were unable to prove that they had used the Big Mac trademark there.

***

Voted one of the world's best restaurants, Osteria Francescana, has a menu item called 'the crunchy part of the lasagna'.

***

Noriyuki "Pat" Morita, who played Mr. Miyagi in the 1984 classic Karate Kid, was 2 years old when he contracted spinal tuberculosis and was confined to a bed in a sanitarium for 9 years. When experimental medicine finally cured him, he was sent to live in an internment camp in Arizona with his family.

***

People who work in silence are slower and less proficient than those who listen to music while working. Video game music itself is designed to keep you motivated and finishing tasks without stealing your focus.

***

Pepperidge Farms produces over 140 billion goldfish crackers each year and nearly 560 million Milano cookies.

***

Despite Millennials often being seen as a 'promiscuous' generation, they have less sexual partners than previous generations and are having less sex than their parents did at the same age.

***

The oldest known musical composition to survive in its entirety is a song called the Epitaph of Seikilos. It was found on a grave in Turkey. Its lyrics "While you live, shine / Have no grief at all / Life exists only for a short while / And time demands its toll."

***

Researchers found that removing trays from college cafeterias reduced the amount of solid food waste by nearly 20%.

***

If you spent one day on each of the islands in the Philippines, it would take you nearly 21 years to visit them all. The latest count of the islands is 7,641.

***

If ripening cherries are not dried after it rains, they will soak up the water, split, and can't be picked and sold. In order to dry them, farmers hire helicopters to slowly maneuver 5 feet over the trees and blasts the water off the cherries!

***

In 2016, a study found that 48% of Thailand's Buddhist monks were overweight. Some temples launched nutritional programs and a local hospital launched a special girdle that tightens around the waist as a gentle reminder.

***

During the 1984 Summer Games in Los Angeles, McDonald's announced a promotion that offered free food and drink every time a U.S. athlete reached the medals podium. The former Soviet Union boycotted the Olympics leading to many American wins and a very costly promotion.

***

In 2013, a Brooklyn school was shut down due to a noxious odor that resulted in several students being transported to the hospital. The odor turned out to be from excessive Axe body spray from some 6th grade boys.

***

SpongeBob SquarePants character Squidward Tentacles has six tentacles, making him neither squid nor octopus. Creator Stephen Hillenberg has stated that he is indeed an octopus.

***

Terry Davis was a schizophrenic programmer who spent 10 years of his life programming a DOS-like operating system called TempleOS. He did so because God told him to build a successor to the Second Temple in the form of an operating system.

***

There are some plants, like the Arabidopsis plant, that emit toxins as a defense mechanism in response to the vibrations of caterpillars chewing - even when the sound is played as a recording.

***

El Azizia in northern Libya held the record for the hottest place on Earth for 90 years, but in 2012, experts reviewing evidence concluded the original reading on the thermometer was taken incorrectly.

***

Roses are planted at the end of a row of grape vines on vineyards because they are very susceptible to powdery mildew and mold. As such, they act as an early warning sign of mold or mildew allowing the vineyard staff to react before it impacts the grapes.

***

The drinking age in Wisconsin is 21, but anyone underage is legally allowed to drink alcohol in bars and restaurants as long as they are with a parent or guardian of legal drinking age and the establishment allows it.

***

Mankind has probed nearly 14 billion miles outward from Earth via Voyager I, but has only drilled 7.5 miles into Earth itself.

***

Actor Jake Gyllenhaal tried out for the part of Frodo in the Lord of the Rings but was not even aware he had to have a British accent for the role, resulting in one of the worst auditions they had.

***

Joseph Stalin had a secret lab that analyzed the poop of foreign leaders in order to build a psychological profile for them.

***

Researchers found that individuals who are anxious are prone to veer to the left when walking because they have more activity in the right hemisphere of the brain.

***

Serial killer Ed Kemper befriended the very police officers investigating his murders and would socialize with them at a bar called the Jury Room. They called him "Big Ed" and never suspected him and thought he was joking when he confessed.

***

The food court at Costco makes so much money selling pizza to hungry shoppers that it ranks as the 14th largest pizza chain in the US. That makes it larger than California Pizza Kitchen and nearly as large as CiCi's.

***

Male human beings produce 1,000,000,000,000,000,000,000,000 times more sperm than females produce eggs.

***

In 2014, some 4,000 black taxi cab drivers brought parts of London to a standstill, protesting against Uber. Ironically, this led to an 850% increase in downloads of Uber on the day.

***

Since 1922, more than 30 cash rewards of up to $1,000,000 have been offered to anyone who can offer proof of the paranormal. To this day, none has ever been collected.

***

Astronauts in space need to sleep near fans so that when they exhale, there isn't a CO_2 cloud in front of their face causing them to potentially suffocate.

***

The red flag, when used by pirates, came to mean "no quarter given", or no mercy would be shown and no life would be spared. Alternatively, a black flag meant that those who surrendered without a fight would be allowed to live.

***

The red-lipped batfish or Galapagos batfish (Ogcocephalus darwini) have frowny-faces and giant red lips. They use their fins as feet to walk around the sea floor because they're terrible swimmers.

***

Scientists estimate there are ~400,000 species of plants on Earth and more than half of them are thought to be edible. However, we as humans only eat about 200 species of plants.

***

Rice is one of the most water-intensive crops to grow, needing about 2,500 liters per kilogram, but this is mainly to prevent weeds. SRI is a trending technique that could cut down the water used by over 50%.

***

In Saudi Arabia, a dozen camels were disqualified from a camel beauty contest for getting Botox injections to make them more attractive.

***

Estádio Milton Corrêa, or Zerão, is a multi-purpose stadium in Northern Brazil situated near the equator or zero degrees latitude and thus has one end in the Northern hemisphere and the other in the Southern.

***

Draco was an Athenian lawyer who gave the city of Athens its first written laws. The word Draconian originated from his name as his laws were so brutal.

***

Old-time 'high-wheeler' bicycles were also known as 'penny farthings', because people thought they looked like the largest (penny) and smallest (farthing) English coins of the day rolling along one after the other.

***

A recent study of biomedical papers published through May 2015 found 213 references "unequivocally citing" Bob Dylan. The singer/songwriter's most popular songs referenced were "The Times They Are a-Changin'," which had 135 citations, and "Blowin' in the Wind," which had 36 citations.

***

The jewel caterpillar (dalceridae) is covered in brightly-colored, translucent spines that make it look like a little pile of gummy candies.

***

It's an urban legend that driving a vehicle barefoot is illegal in the US. None of the states have a law that requires you to be wearing footwear while driving.

***

Artist Max Siedentopf is creating an installation called "Toto Forever" at an undisclosed location somewhere in the Namib Desert, Africa. The solar powered installation will consist of six speakers and an MP3 player with Toto's Africa on repeat.

***

Women are better at discerning shades of colors, while men are better at tracking fast-moving objects and identifying detail from a distance. These are evolutionary details linked to our hunter-gatherer past.

***

Climate change is turning the world's oldest mummies into black goo. For 7,000 years, these mummies have survived in Chile's Atacama Desert, but humidity in the area has risen enough to cause rapid mummy decomposition.

***

Researchers traveled to Antarctica and put 10 king penguins on a treadmill. They found fat king penguins are more unsteady on their feet while waddling compared to their slimmer counterparts.

***

A disgruntled businessman in Vermont, who was upset with the local officials for denying a building permit for his proposed business, got revenge by building a giant, illuminated middle finger statue on his property at a cost of ~$4,000.

***

Dr. Barry J. Marshall proved to the medical community that ulcers weren't caused by stomach acid by drinking Helicobacter pylori bacterium. He developed stomach ulcers within days, treated them with antibiotics, and went on to win a Nobel Prize.

***

Wellington boots were oddly enough designed by Germans, named by an Irishman, manufactured by an American in France and first worn by French peasants.

***

Esperanto is a constructed international auxiliary language based on a mix of English, German, French, and Spanish. It has just 16 rules and each letter has only one pronunciation. It was created in 1887 by the Polish doctor L. L. Zamenhof.

***

In 1964, when Bob Dylan first met The Beatles, he had misheard the lyrics to I Want to Hold Your Hand as "I get high" instead of "I can't hide", and showed up to meet them ready to smoke. He gave a joint to Ringo, who didn't realize he was supposed to pass it and smoked the whole thing himself.

***

Penguin colonies generate so much poop that it stains the ice and allows scientists to track their movement and colony size using satellite imagery.

***

Hygiene standards were so low that the official 2019 Yu-Gi-Oh tournament hosted by Konami instituted a hygiene clause to the rule book. This allows judges to penalize players with dirty clothing or terrible odor by giving them a loss.

***

Studies have shown that removing lead from gasoline is one of the factors that lead to the drop in the violent crime rate in America in the 1990s. Individuals exposed to lead at young ages have numerous conditions and problems with impulse control, all of which may negatively impact decision making and lead to a life of violent crime as they reach adulthood.

***

The word sarcasm can be traced back to the Greek verb sarkazein, which initially meant "to tear flesh like a dog."

***

In 1979, when the Skylab re-entry approached and headed for Australia, the San Francisco Examiner offered $10,000 to the first person to deliver a piece to them within 72 hours. A 17yr old Aussie collected a piece, jumped on a plane to SFO with no passport or luggage, and collected his prize.

***

In the late 1600s, London was plagued by a sexual attacker, dubbed 'Whipping Tom', who would spank his victims with his hand or sometimes a rod and shout 'Spanko!' before running away.

***

Japan has installed special concrete tunnels under some of their train tracks to allow for turtles to cross the tracks.

***

There's a species of orchid that looks like a monkey's face called 'Dracula Simia'. It is native to the tropical cloud forests of Southeastern Ecuador and Peru as it grows best in elevations above 2,000 feet.

***

Recent research found that nearly half of all US food produced is discarded (left in the field to rot, fed to livestock, or hauled directly from the field to landfill) because of unrealistic "cosmetic food" standards.

***

Tartle is an old Scottish word for the moment of hesitation when you are introducing someone whose name you can't remember.

***

Leonardo da Vinci is often credited with being the first to introduce the idea of contact lenses in his 1508 Codex of the eye, Manual D. However, his ideas for implementing the lenses was entirely impractical.

***

In 1999, Philip Morris attempted to convince the Czech Republic that smoking was highly beneficial to the country, as more people would die earlier, saving the government millions on pensions, hospitals, and housing for elderly citizens.

***

The second part of the 25th amendment deals specifically with procedures for a President who is unfit to serve. It has been used three times, all related to colon issues and two of the three were a result of Presidential colonoscopies.

***

Rats are nonemetic, meaning they can't vomit. It is why rat poison is so effective. They also can't burp and they don't experience heartburn.

***

The tradition of firing guns as a salute was originally a sign of peaceful intentions. Since guns and cannons would need to be reloaded after each shot, firing your gun in the air essentially rendered you "unarmed."

***

Mary, or Maryam in Islam, is mentioned more frequently in the Qur'an than she is in the Holy Bible. Mary is the only woman named in the Qur'an and the 19th chapter is even named for her (Surat Maryam).

***

A rescue dog in Mexico named Frida saved the lives of 12 people who were trapped under rubble due to earthquakes. She identified a total of 52 bodies during her career. Now retired, she is a national heroine in Mexico with a statue and all.

***

Fidel Castro, the Cuban dictator who died at age 90, slept with ~35,000 women, smoked his first cigar at age 14, and believed he survived nearly 600 assassination attempts.

***

The Statue of Liberty's original concept was titled "Egypt Carrying the Light to Asia" depicting a Muslim peasant woman (fellah) guarding the Suez Canal. A 180 ft tall lighthouse was built instead.

***

In 1947, Thor Heyerdahl, a Norwegian adventurer and scientist, sailed 5,000 miles across the Pacific in a hand-built raft (known as the Kon-Tiki Expedition to prove the ancients could've accomplished this too.

***

A group of unicorns is called a blessing.

***

According to research, up to 50% of the Asian population lack a specific enzyme found in the liver to metabolize alcohol.

***

In 2013, the United States surpassed Russia and Saudi Arabia and now produces more oil and natural gas than any other country in the world.

***

John List killed his entire family in 1971. The murders were so precisely planned, it took a month for anyone to notice. He was finally caught in 1989, after a forensic artist created a lifelike bust of him which appeared on America's Most Wanted.

***

On March 14, 1942, Anne Miller, diagnosed with blood poisoning, was given a tablespoon of penicillin, one half of the entire stockpile of the antibiotic in the whole United States.

***

In 1821, an African American business owner named Thomas Jennings invented the dry-cleaning process and was one of the first African Americans to be granted a patent. He used the proceeds from his invention to buy his wife and children out of slavery.

***

Volunteers spent 2 years cleaning up over 11,500,000 pounds of trash along Mumbai's Versova beach in one of 'the world's largest beach clean-ups', resulting in Olive Ridley turtles returning to lay eggs for the first time in 20 years.

***

The US's Center for Disease Control has a Center for Preparedness and Response which includes specific guidance for zombie preparedness.

***

In 1959, police were called to a segregated library in S. Carolina when 9yr-old Ronald McNair refused to leave. He later got a PhD in Physics from MIT and died in 1986 aboard the space shuttle Challenger. The library that refused to lend him books is now named after him.

***

Two actors have died while playing Judas in live Biblical plays by accidentally hanging themselves for real during the death scene.

***

On the Queen of England's birthday in 2015, she was given a gift of £5,000 worth of stud sperm by horse breeder Christina Patino.

***

The price of a college textbook increased 90% from 1998 to 2016, while recreational book prices fell by more than 35% over the same time period.

***

During the US prohibition era, moonshiners would wear cow shoes. The fancy footwear left hoofprints instead of footprints, helping distillers and smugglers evade police.

***

Recently, a British Airways Boeing 747 set a new subsonic record for a flight between New York's JFK and London's Heathrow airports. The jumbo jet maxed out at 825 mph while riding a 200-mph jet stream tailwind to arrive in 4 hours and 56 minutes.

***

Walt Disney World once had its own airport with a singing runway (Lake Buena Vista STOLPort runway). Grooves in the tarmac were spaced so the lines played the opening notes of "When You Wish Upon a Star". The airport closed in 1972.

***

Vesna Vulović was a Serbian flight attendant who was the only survivor after JAT Flight 367 exploded on January 26, 1972. As a result, she holds the world record for surviving the highest fall without a parachute. She fell over 33,000 feet while trapped in the fuselage.

***

While playing a 3-minute blitz game of chess at the World Championships in 2019, grandmaster Magnus Carlsen wasted 20 seconds of his time taking his suit coat off, drinking water, and organizing his pieces - and still won.

***

Francis Pegahmagabow was a Canadian indigenous man who fought in WWI. He killed 378 enemies with his Ross rifle and captured another 300, making him one of the most successful marksmen in WWI.

***

A recent study found elephants console one another when they are upset with gentle touches and trunk strokes. Previously, only humans, great apes, and birds in the raven family were known to do this.

***

A 2015 study in the UK found that 72% of 18 to 25-year-olds believe it's easier to communicate their feelings with emojis rather than it is with words.

***

On NASA's Gemini XII flight, the computer docking system failed and Buzz Aldrin (who did his doctoral thesis at MIT on line-of-sight orbital mechanics) successfully calculated the docking trajectory using a sextant and a slide rule.

***

The center of the Milky Way tastes like raspberries and smells like Captain Morgan. Astronomers researching the giant dust cloud in the middle of the galaxy found the chemical ethyl formate, which gives raspberries their flavor and smells like rum.

***

In Roald Dahl's Charlie and Chocolate Factory, the Oompa-Loompas where at one point known as Whipple-Scrumpets.

***

At one point in the 1990's, 50% of all Compact Discs production in the world was dedicated solely to creating AOL install/sign-up discs. They spent over $300 million on discs and acquired a new subscriber every six seconds.

***

The Omeo is a wheelchair based on Segway technology which allows users to move hands-free at a max speed of 20km per hour.

***

Edgar Allan Poe's bestselling book as a living author was a schoolbook he was hired to abridge and reorganize titled The Conchologist's First Book.

***

Incredibly, recycling just one ton of paper saves 3.3 cubic yards of landfill space, 17 mature trees, 682.5 gallons of oil and 7000 gallons of water.

***

Grammy award winning Jamaican rapper Shaggy, famous for his hits "It Wasn't Me" and "Boombastic", served as a US Marine in Operation Desert Storm during the First Persian Gulf War.

***

A 2015 study from the University of Innsbruck found that people who drink their coffee black are more likely to be psychopaths.

***

The drunkard's cloak was a barrel with holes for one's head and arms that was put on drunk people to publicly shame them while they were paraded through their town. Historical records show the punishment was used in the UK, USA, Netherlands and Denmark.

***

Venetian 17th century scientist Michiel Angelo Salamon came up with an idea to distill the essence of the bubonic plague and paint it onto Albanian fezzes which the besieging Turks would acquire.

***

According to scientists from the Defense Advanced Research Laboratory (DARPA), bees or buzzing insects can be trained to detect bombs.

***

The world's most prolific gin drinkers are Filipinos. The Philippines accounts for 43% of the world's gin consumption and they mostly drink the locally produced Ginebra San Miguel.

***

Despite cacao being around for thousands of years, the first solid chocolate bar wasn't produced until the 1840's. It was previously consumed in a powder or drink form.

***

According to the "Regulation of Traditions and Customs in the Republic of Tajikistan," □ which were introduced in 2007 and updated in 2017, the celebration of birthdays anywhere except in the privacy of the family circle is strictly forbidden and carries a hefty fine if caught.

***

A Calvin and Hobbes comic from 1992 referred to the start of the universe as the "Horrendous Space Kablooie" (or HSK) because they thought "The Big Bang" was too boring. The term has since become popular among scientists and has been included in books and university courses.

***

In 2008, Elon Musk had to borrow money from friends to pay rent after he invested all US$180 million earned from the sale of PayPal to eBay on his three ventures SpaceX, Tesla and Solar City.

***

The shortest nation in Europe is Malta. The Maltese have an average height of 164.9 cm (~65 in) compared with the EU average of 169.6 cm (~67 in).

***

There is an estimated 5% of the population that has never experienced a headache.

***

A form of lasers called 'optical tweezers' uses two beams of light to squeeze and manipulate objects as small as a single atom.

***

In 2016, there were 870 Chinese-licensed "living Buddhas," searchable by name, temple and identity card number or "living-Buddha card number." The license process aims to help cut down on fraud.

***

After being denied permission to construct a building on an empty lot, a London man applied for a permit for a tank. The council approved thinking it was a septic tank. Instead the man bought a Russian T-34 tank, parked it on his property and pointed the gun towards the city planning office.

***

Gibbons start each day by singing at sunrise. Their vocalizations are often referred to as 'song' because of the way they modulate their pitch as well as singing with others in 'duets.'

***

Until 1937, it was illegal for men to be topless in the US - even on beaches. The fine was $1 if caught in New York City or its municipal beaches.

***

Some lizards have a visible third eye known as a parietal eye, which is an opalescent gray spot on the top of their heads. The eye is sensitive to changes in light & dark but cannot form images.

***

A new microbe called a hemimastigote was found in Nova Scotia. The Hemimastix kukwesjijk is not a plant, animal, fungus, or protozoa. It constitutes an entirely new kingdom, a new branch on the tree of life.

***

There are 12 copies of the Gutenberg Bible which were printed on vellum. Each of these copy's required ~170 calf hides.

***

In 1936, Cleveland lost the largest book in the world. The Golden Book of Cleveland was 7 feet by 5 feet and 3 feet thick, with 6,000 pages - about the size of a queen-size bed. It weighed ~2 1/2 tons.

***

The highest crime rate per capita of any city in the world is at Vatican City where an average of 600 crimes (primarily petty theft) are committed per year, despite only having 800 residents.

***

Ronald Reagan enjoyed the White House's squirrel population so much that on his last day in office he left a sign for them warning them to beware of George H.W. Bush's dog.

***

75% of the earth's population, an estimated 4 billion people, have no address for mailing purposes.

***

A man once sued a dry cleaner store for $67 million over a late return of a pair of $1000 pants. He reduced it to $45 million in court. The case was thrown out multiple times and the man, a judge himself, lost his job for a lack of "judicial temperament."

***

When morphine was first isolated from opium in 1805, one of its early uses was as a "non-addictive" drug to treat people with an addiction to the relatively less addictive opium.

***

A popular additive to many perfumes, Ambergris, comes from the intestines of sperm whales. When it's fresh, not surprisingly, it smells like crap, but then later begins to smell sweet and 'earthy'.

***

The Mexican Constitution of 1917 was the first document in history that said every person has the right to an education.

***

The first woman appearing on a US postage stamp was Queen Isabella of Spain, honoring her patronage of Christopher Columbus's voyage to the Americas.

***

Blue M&Ms didn't exist until 1995, when a poll was held to replace the tan color M&M that was deemed redundant because of the brown M&M.

***

The Kumbh Mela (or Grand Pitcher Festival) is a huge Hindu religious festival that takes place in India every 12 years. In 2001, 60 million people attended, breaking the record for the world's biggest gathering.

***

In 1960, Col. Joseph Kittinger set the then world record for the highest skydive at just over 19 miles. During free fall, he reached a speed of 614 mph, nearly the speed of sound. His record was finally broken by his mentee in 2012

***

Mantis shrimps' eyes are more evolved than those of humans: they have four times as many color receptors and can see UV, visible, and polarized light.

***

Papua New Guinea is the most linguistically diverse country in the world with 851 individual languages listed.

***

The space shuttle flew 135 missions with a flight computer that had less than 1% of the computing power of Microsoft's Xbox 360 game console.

***

During the California gold rush, a slice of bread cost $1 or $2 if you wanted it buttered. That's the equivalent of over $28 and $56 today.

***

Ama or uminchu, are female Japanese pearl divers that start diving at the age of 12-13 and are sometimes active into their 70s. They free dive with only a wetsuit and a traditional headscarf. They have a unique and defining technique in which they release air in a long whistle as they resurface.

***

A 2015 study by Clear Labs found that 10% of vegetarian hot dogs sold in the US had meat in them. An additional 2% contained human DNA.

***

The Cosmic Crisp Apple was researched and developed for 22 years by WSU's tree fruit breeding program. It will stay fresh for up to 10 months in a fridge while still maintaining its deliciously sweet and tangy flavor.

***

The Incas used colorful knotted cords called Quipu to record numbers and archives such as census data, tax obligations, and storehouse records. They had up to a thousand unique strands.

***

According to the USDA, a sandwich must contain at least 35% cooked meat but no more than 50% bread.

***

In medieval games of chess, pawns that had been promoted to a queen would be given the title of "advisor," so as to not imply that the king had more than one queen or was unfaithful.

***

The first Deadpool movie was only greenlit after test footage shot by the directors two years earlier was leaked online. The identity of who leaked it at 20th Century Fox remains a mystery.

***

Recent studies show that Americans eat 1 out of every 5 meals in their vehicles.

***

The beautiful Yunhe rice terraced fields in Zhejiang province are the largest terraced fields in Eastern China. They are situated at an altitude between 200 to 1,400 meters and have been feeding locals for over 1000 years.

***

Binky the polar bear lived in Anchorage's Alaska Zoo. He mauled two visitors who jumped over the safety rails on separate occasions. After the maulings, Binky merchandise was sold with the slogan "Send another tourist, this one got away".

***

The wingless midge (or small fly) Belgica Antarctica is the largest land animal permanently living in Antarctica is only .24 inches long.

***

Violets can be smelled for only a few moments at a time because they get their scent from ionone which shuts the smell receptors off after simulating them. After a few breaths the scent pops up again.

***

Milton Hershey didn't have any children so he opened an orphanage school and left his entire fortune including majority ownership of Hershey Chocolate Company in a trust for the school. 70% of the company is still owned by Milton Hershey School.

***

In the 1920's, Hugo Gernsback invented The Isolator which was a helmet aimed to improve concentration by blocking out noise and narrowing the user's field of view.

***

Nike had a clause in Michael Jordan's record rookie contract: be rookie of the year, average 20 points per game, be an all-star, or sell $4 mill worth shoes in a year. Jordan became rookie of the year, scored 28.2 points per game, named all-star, and Nike sold $100 mill of shoes in 1984-85.

***

Over 960 bamboo slips from the Han Dynasty (206 BC - AD 25) were found with more than 25,000 characters detailing basic theories of traditional Chinese medicine, acupuncture, prescription, as well as a book on law.

***

The Nilotic peoples Nuer, Dinka, and Atuot of South Sudan occasionally sacrifice a cucumber instead of an ox.

***

The Moscow mule drink was created by John Martin who couldn't sell his vodka, Jack Morgan couldn't sell his ginger beer, and a mystery lady that had too many copper mugs.

***

The Norway national soccer team is the only national team that has never lost a match against Brazil. Moreover, Norway has won two matches against Brazil and tied two.

***

A quarter of a million people in Denmark gather on "Organic Day" in April to watch the cows being let out to pasture. For some 20 minutes, the cows seem to "dance" in the fields.

***

Common snapping turtles have no teeth but they can produce 1000 PSI bite force with their sharp beak and firm jaws, which is more than enough to bite off a finger.

***

A British teenager went blind after maintaining a poor diet for several years, which consisted only of French fries, Pringles, white bread, and the occasional slice of ham or sausage.

***

Since 1973, Volkswagen has manufactured currywurst at its Wolfsburg plant. The sausage is branded as a "Volkswagen Original Part' with its own part number. They produce nearly 7 million currywurst yearly, which is more than the number of cars they produce across all their factories.

***

The shortest war on record was fought between Zanzibar and England in 1896. Zanzibar surrendered after 38 minutes and some 500 casualties.

***

Arnold Schwarzenegger wasn't allowed to dub his own role in Terminator to German, as his accent is considered very rural by German/Austrian standards and it would be too ridiculous to have a death machine from the future sound like a hillbilly.

***

Snoopy used the phrase 'Cowabunga!' in the 1950's, long before the Teenage Mutant Ninja Turtles used it as their catchphrase in the 1980's.

***

Sloths poop once a week. This is the only reason they will leave their tree. It's always a life-threatening situation for them as predators can easily prey on them while they do their "poo dance" at ground level.

***

There are more than 7500 tomato varieties grown around the world. Over 175 million tons are produced globally each year with China producing the most of any country at ~32% of total worldwide tomatoes grown.

***

An actual chill pill, which could even be made at home, was used in the late 1800's to remedy chills associated with a high fever.

***

The tongue is a unique organ exhibiting many static and dynamic characteristics which differ considerably between individuals. Tongue prints are as unique as fingerprints.

***

Christopher Langan, one of the smartest people in the world according to his IQ test results, spent 20 years as a bouncer on Long Island while he worked on his Cognitive-Theoretic Model of the Universe.

***

The popular idiom "over and out" from TV and movies makes no sense in actual radio communications because "over" means you want a reply and "out" means you do not expect a reply.

***

There are no bridges over the Amazon river despite it being the second longest river in the world.

***

Around New Year and before Lent, those in Bulgarian kukeri costumes walk and dance through villages to scare away evil spirits with their costumes and the sound of their bells.

***

The band Chumbawamba holds the world record for the longest album title at 156 words and 857 characters long for 2008 album "The Boy Bands Have Won..."

***

"The Powerpuff Girls" was originally called "Whoopass Stew!" Rather than adding Chemical X to his formula, Professor Utonium accidentally adds a can of whoop ass and creates The Whoopass Girls.

***

Physicist William Higinbotham worked on both the first nuclear bomb and what some consider to be the first video game ever, 'Tennis for Two.'

***

In 2015, Tara, the tabby cat, won the SPCA Los Angeles's annual national Hero Dog Award for tackling a dog attacking a child.

***

Ducks can keep their eyes open underwater due to a transparent third, sideways eyelid called a nictating membrane or haw. All birds have it and even humans have a vestigial remnant called the plica semilunaris.

***

There is a version of the Mexican song La Cucaracha sang by Poncho Villa's troops in battle during the Mexican Revolution that is about a cockroach that can't walk because it doesn't have marijuana to smoke.

***

Galeanthropy is a mental condition of thinking that one has become a cat, which is usually manifested in the adoption of feline mannerisms and habits.

***

The Parthian shot, an ancient military tactic where archers on horses would feign retreat and then turn their bodies while at full gallop to shoot at the pursuing enemy.

***

Arnold Schwarzenegger paid Austria $20,000 to ship him a 1951 M-47 Patton tank, the exact same tank he drove when he was a soldier. It is fully operable (minus the gun) and he uses it to support his fundraising efforts.

***

The USSR successfully sent a spacecraft and entry probe to Venus in 1966 becoming the first space probe to hit the surface of another planet - three years before the US put man on the moon.

***

The builders of Japan's Nijo castle created purposefully squeaky floors, known as nightingale floors, to prevent ninja assassins from sneaking in. The floors were designed so that just the lightest step produced a clearly audible sound warning the guards.

***

Thurl Ravenscroft was both the singer of 'You're a Mean One, Mr. Grinch' and also the voice of Frosted Flakes mascot Tony The Tiger.

***

If you were on the moon, the Earth wouldn't actually move in the sky. It would appear to wobble a little because the moon is elliptical but it would never "rise" or "set".

***

Mary Shelley's favorite keepsake was her dead husband and poet Percy Shelly's heart. After the death of her husband, the Frankenstein author carried his heart with her in a silken shroud for almost 30 years until she died in 1851.

***

Italy's top civil court ruled that restaurants must disclose to their customers if they serve frozen food or it's considered commercial fraud

***

A meteorwrong is a rock that is believed to be a meteorite, but is in fact just a rock that is terrestrial in origin, also known as a pseudometeorite.

***

Switzerland is the only country in the world which could fit more than its entire population into bunkers in case of an emergency.

***

According to new findings, in one ancient South American culture, some babies wore burial headgear made from other children's skulls.

***

The term "noon" is derived from the Latin nona hora or ninth hour. The medieval monastic day began at 6 a.m. making the ninth hour actually 3 p.m. The meaning of the word slowly shifted to midday/12:00 p.m. between the 12th and 14th centuries.

***

When DMA Design/Rockstar Games first released Grand Theft Auto, they actually paid reviewers to negatively review the game in order to keep it controversial and thus popular. They planted articles in right wing newspapers to ensure moral outrage and drive the game to success.

***

In Welsh, the word for week is wythnos, which literally means "eight-nights". Historically, the week started and ended with night.

***

Napoleon Bonaparte's penis was removed from his dead body during autopsy, displayed at a museum, and eventually sold for $2,700 in the 1970s.

***

After 13 years of trying to find the structure of a protein, scientists created an online competitive game called Foldit that asked gamers to try and solve it. The structure was then found in 3 weeks.

***

The Crooked Forest is located in Poland and is home to hundreds of pine trees planted in the 1930's which are mysteriously curved at a 90° angle.

***

The Ethiopian calendar is ~7 years behind the Gregorian calendar due to them having a 13th month of either 5 or 6 days (in the case of a leap year). They celebrated the new millennium on Sept. 12, 2007.

***

The term "plastic surgery" was coined in 1839, 70 years before plastic was even invented. It comes from the Greek word "plastike" which means "the art of modelling" of malleable flesh.

***

The longest-serving prisoner in American history was Paul Geidel, who served 68 years and 245 days between 1911 and 1980 for second degree murder. He was first incarcerated at age 17 and finally released at age 86.

***

Thunder-plump is an early 19th century Scottish word meaning a heavy and sudden shower of rain accompanied by thunder and lightning.

***

In 1975, the mummified body of bank robber Elmer McCurdy was found in an amusement park by a TV crew. It had been mistaken for a wax mannequin, and was only found out after a man moved it and its arm fell off, exposing human bone. Elmer died in 1911.

***

The Scatophagus argus, which translates to "spotted feces-eater", is a fish more commonly called the spotted scat that is known for its indiscriminate eating habits.

***

Titanoboa was a prehistoric snake that lived about 60 million years ago. It could grow up to 42 feet long and weigh around 2500 lb.

***

Male giant jewel beetles (Julodimorpha bakewelli) often prefer to mate with beer bottles instead of female jewel beetles due to the beer bottle's large size and attractive coloring.

***

Stanford researchers developed a new battery that harnesses "blue energy" from mixing salt and fresh water. Every cubic meter of freshwater that mixes with seawater produces ~.65 kilowatt-hours of energy, enough to power the average house for about 30 minutes.

***

Researchers from the University of Washington found that when the moon is directly overhead, it's gravitational pull on the clouds results in less rain.

***

Cincinnati, Ohio has a subway system over 2 miles in length that was built in the early 1900's but never used and has been left abandoned ever since.

***

Ada Lovelace, considered one of the first computer programmers, wrote a theory of "flyology" on powered flight that accurately documented wing-body ratios to achieve flight. She was 12 years old when she published it.

***

In 2011, an iPhone 4 fell out of a skydiver's pocket and fell ~13500 ft, landing on top of the building a half mile away. The iPhone was still able to be located via its GPS signal as well as receive phone calls.

***

Hawaii allows people to throw their beloved's ashes into their volcanoes, as long as you pay a $25 permit and do it discretely.

***

Rolling Stone magazine originally gave Nirvana's Nevermind a 3-star rating in 1991. They now give it 5 stars and rank it as the 17th greatest album of all time.

***

There are only six full-time skywriters, those who use aircraft to expel special smoke during flight in patterns that create readable words from the ground, left in the world.

***

In 2013, Disney abandoned its policy of letting disabled people skip lines in its theme parks, after rampant abuse of the rule by people hiring disabled "tour guides" to skip waiting lines for rides. These guides sometimes charged up to hundreds of dollars per hour.

***

According to the CIA's 2013 data, the United States has 13,513 airports (recognizable from the air), which is more than the next 10 countries combined.

***

One-armed tennis player Hans Redl played at Wimbledon from 1947 to 1956. He served by tossing the ball up with his racket.

***

Photographer Robert Landsberg was taking photographs during the Mount St. Helens eruption in 1980. Upon realizing he wouldn't survive, he lied down on top of his equipment to preserve the photographs he had taken of the event.

***

The idea that breakfast is the most important meal of the day came from General Foods trying to sell more grape nuts cereal during its 1944 marketing campaign.

***

The scientific name for the dark kangaroo mouse is Microdipodops megacephalus, meaning "two small feet with a big head".

***

The International Potato Center has successfully grown potatoes in a simulated Mars environment. They grew the plants at the same air pressure and atmosphere as on Mars, and used saline desert soils analogous to Martian soils as the growing medium.

***

Slugs have roughly 27,000 teeth. They routinely wear out and then lose them, but replace them by moving their back rows of teeth forward.

***

Cuddling with a partner can significantly relieve pain and improve the healing of wounds due to the increased release in oxytocin.

***

Villagers in central China have long been using dinosaur bones in medicine and soups, thinking they were from dragons.

***

Glitter is terrible for the environment. Most glitter products are made from plastic, which contributes to the problem of microplastics in our oceans. These microplastics can harm marine life by releasing chemicals that disrupt animal hormones.

***

Belgium is the world's leading producer and exporter of billiard balls thanks to the Saluc company, which has been producing the balls made of phenolic resin since ~1960.

***

Tim Wong, a 28-year-old aquatic biologist from northern California, has single-handedly repopulated the rare California Pipevine Swallowtail butterfly species in his backyard!

***

When the Six Flags Over Texas theme park opened in 1961, it had a section dedicated to the Confederacy where actors would hunt through the crowd for Union "spies" and "execute" them by firing squad. Boys and girls could also sign up to defend the South as soldiers and nurses.

***

Peru is home to ~3800 different types of potatoes, having been domesticated there some ~10,000 years ago. They differ in size, shape, color, skin, pulp, texture, and taste.

***

Ferdinand Cheval was a French mailman who spent 33 years building a palace with stones he collected on his mail route. Le Palais idéal ("Ideal Palace") is regarded as an extraordinary example of naïve art architecture.

***

Grigori Perelman is the only person in history to have solved one of the seven Millennium Prize Problems. After solving the Poincaré conjecture Perelman was offered both Field's Medal and $1 million prize money, he declined them both.

***

British politician Philip Noel-Baker is the only person to have won an Olympic medal (silver in the 1500m) and a Nobel (Peace) Prize.

***

The Mongols never took baths or washed their clothes, fearing that it would contaminate the water and infuriate the dragons responsible for controlling the water cycles.

***

Millennials between the ages of 18-34 are more likely to live with their parents instead of a spouse/partner. This is the first time this has been true of this age demographic since record-keeping began in the 1880s.

***

During WW2, the U.S. Navy diving manual contained detailed instructions on how to release oneself from the grasp of a giant clam by severing its adductor muscles close to its shell.

***

Researchers recently demonstrated that twig-mimicking caterpillars of the peppered moth can sense a twig's color with their skin. Caterpillars that were blindfolded changed the color of their bodies to match their background.

***

Hotel La Montaña Mágica is a unique hotel built to mimic a volcano and even erupts water. It sits deep within the depths of the private Huilo-Huilo biological reserve in Chile.

***

The UK Royal Navy's nuclear submarines run on a variant of Windows XP dubbed 'Windows for Submarines'. Its actual name is Submarine Command System New Generation or 'SMCS NG'.

***

Charles Vance Millar, a rich Canadian financier, made his will one last practical joke. In it, he left three men who hated each other a joint lifetime tenancy in a villa, some protestant ministers $700,000 in Catholic beer stock, and anti-horse racing advocates $25,000 in Jockey club stock.

***

Russian Lyudmila Pavlichenko aka "Lady Death" was the most lethal female sniper in history, she went on to record 309 confirmed kills in WWll.

***

North Korea has only 8 internet hosts while the Vatican City has 107. USA has the most out of any country with over 500 million.

***

Roosters have "built-in" earplugs, which prevents them from damaging their hearing as they crow. When roosters open their beaks fully, their external auditory canals close completely.

***

Wat Pa Maha Chedi Kaew (Wilderness Temple of the Great Glass Pagoda) is a Buddhist temple in Thailand and is also known as the Temple of a Million Bottles because it's constructed with ~1.5 million empty Heineken and Chang beer bottles.

***

The concept of "the munchies", a side-effect from the use of Cannabis and it's active ingredient THC's impact on the CB1 receptor which results in an increase in appetite, has been understood since ~300 BC.

***

In 2013, the town of Brunete near Madrid had volunteers watch for dog owners who didn't pick up their dog's poop, gather the owner's information by petting the dogs, and then sent the poop to their home in a "lost property" box.

***

University of Melbourne Archaeologists have discovered 15 new sites in Laos containing more than one hundred 1000-year-old massive stone jars possibly used to "bury" the dead.

***

Since most meerkat "mobs" have only a single dominant pair reproducing, they have eating (or growing) contests to establish who is the next dominant female in the hierarchy.

***

During WW1, many dogs were trained as 'casualty' or 'mercy' dogs. They would seek out the injured and carry them medical supplies, or wait with the mortally wounded.

***

Birds eat up to 550 million tons of insects each year or as many as 20 quadrillion (20,000,000,000,000,000) individual bugs.

***

In 2010, Dr. Elena Bodnar created the "Emergency Bra" which can be unhooked and split into two face masks which filter out harmful chemicals.

***

One bite from a Lone Star tick can cause alpha-gal syndrome, which makes you allergic to red meat.

***

The Guinness world record for the largest snowflake was a snowflake 15 inches in diameter and 8 inches thick recorded at Fort Keogh, Montana in 1887.

***

Researchers found during the 2017 North American eclipse that bees don't buzz during an eclipse. The bees were active and noisy right up until the last moments before totality. As totality hit, the bees all went silent in unison.

***

In 1955, Federal agents arrested John Gilbert Graham for blowing up an airplane but learned that it was not in fact a federal crime to blow up an airplane. Colorado instead charged him for the murder of his mother, a passenger on the plane.

***

The carnivorous harp sponge (Chondrocladia lyra) traps its prey in its hooks and then secretes a digestive membrane which breaks it down cell by cell and absorbs it through its pores.

***

Kale, collard greens, Chinese broccoli, cauliflower, cabbage, Brussels sprouts, and broccoli all come from the same plant: brassica oleracea. They are just different breeds or cultivars.

***

In Japan, businesses like banks & convenience stores visibly keep baseball-sized orange orbs behind the counter. These "anticrime color balls" are filled with bright pigment that burst on impact & are for employees to throw at robbers to improve the chance of arrest.

***

The killers of Eden or Twofold Bay killers were a pod of orcas in SE Australia which helped local whalers kill baleen whales between 1840 and 1930. The arrangement became known as the "law of the tongue" because the whalers would leave the carcass for the orcas to eat the lips and tongues.

***

Archaeologists found "chewing gum" in western Sweden believed to be 9,000 years old, made of resin sweetened with honey, and the tooth marks showed it had been chewed on by a stone-age teenager.

***

Despite it being common practice for casinos to ban card counters, a 1979 New Jersey Supreme Court decision banned all Atlantic City casinos from doing so, making them the only state in America where they can't throw out skilled blackjack players.

***

Uganda is home to more than half of the world's total population of mountain gorillas. Approximately 400 mountain gorillas live in Bwindi Impenetrable National Park.

***

Some animals and insects, like squirrels and bumblebees, use a "mating plug" to prevent other males from inseminating females they have already mated with.

***

Up until 2000, Walmart took out life insurance policies on their employees and kept the payouts when they died, a practice known as "dead peasant insurance."

***

In 2013, NASA's Mars Curiosity rover hummed Happy Birthday to itself by vibrating its sample-analysis unit to the musical tune, but did so only on its first "birthday".

***

There are four glass platforms suspended 1,353 feet in the air, located on the Willis Tower's 103rd floor Skydeck. The observation perches have walls, floors, and ceilings made entirely of glass.

***

The Metropolitan Museum of Art in New York holds the world's oldest piano. The piano dates back to 1720 and was one of Bartolomeo Cristofori's (inventor of the piano) earliest creations.

***

James Christopher Harrison is an Australian blood donor whose rare plasma composition has helped in the treatment of Rhesus disease. In May 2018, he made his final donation (1173rd) at the age of 81 after having saved 2.4m babies during his lifetime as a donor.

***

There are silverfish in the desert that don't need to drink as they can absorb moisture from the air through their anus.

***

The first empirical study on "dick pics" found that 48% of men have sent unsolicited pictures of their genitals. Those men who send unsolicited pictures are also bigger narcissists and more sexist than their counterparts.

***

The Observer was the world's first Sunday newspaper. It was first published on December 4, 1791 by W.S. Bourne. It was unprofitable and soon became subsidized by the government, thus losing their editorial independence.

***

WD-40 is named as such because it was the 40th formulation that finally worked for the fledgling Rocket Chemical Company. The "WD" simply stands for water displacement.

***

The profane Hungarian response to being given an unreasonably large workload is "bekergettek tatott szajjal a faszerdobe," or "They chased me into the dick-forest with a wide-open mouth."

***

A 2016 Cornell study found that you are four times more likely to order dessert if your waiter or waitress was overweight.

***

Cockroaches can live for several weeks without their heads because their brains are located inside their body. However, they would eventually die from being unable to eat.

***

Qian Xuesen, a Chinese rocket scientist and mathematician, worked on the Manhattan Project during WW2 to help America build the world's first atomic bomb. During the Cold War, he was accused of being a communist and fled to China, where he helped China build its first atomic bomb.

***

In 2007, archaeologists discovered the oldest known wine-making facility in the world. It was found within a cave (Areni-1) near Areni in present-day Armenia and dates back 6100 years.

***

When squirrels have spare nuts, they bury them, digging a separate hole for each. However, researchers found that up to 20% of the time they are elaborately faking burying nuts to trick would-be thieves.

***

Amelia Earhart rejected her eventual husband, George Putnam's, marriage proposals five times and finally accepted the sixth offer but agreed only to a temporary, one-year marriage to test the feasibility of the relationship.

***

For over the past 20 years, Lithuania has held an annual crawling race for babies. The babies are aged between seven months and a year and compete in heats along a five-meter, carpeted track.

***

Ice cream originated in China, as early as 3000 BC. The original recipe consisted of milk, rice and snow. King Tang of Shang, had 94 ice men who helped to make the dish of buffalo milk, flour and camphor.

***

Turkish artist Hasan Kale paints miniature pictures on foods such as; peanuts, pumpkin seeds, almonds, banana slices, chocolates, and many more. Due to the size of his canvases, he uses a magnifying glass while painting.

***

After the breakup of the Soviet Union, the Lithuanian basketball team couldn't afford to participate in the 1992 Olympics. The Grateful Dead funded the team's expenses and designed some tie-dye gear which they wore to accept their Bronze medal.

***

Boys born in winter are more likely to be left-handed than those born during the rest of the year in what scientists say is indirect evidence of hormonal mechanism.

***

It is illegal under German law to deny the holocaust occurred and is punishable by up to 5 years in prison.

***

An asthmatic otter named Mishka has learned how to use an AeroKat inhaler to help deal with asthma attacks.

***

Tea symbolizes loyalty, love and happily married life in Chinese weddings because tea trees cannot be transplanted - they will only grow and sprout from a seed.

***

According to cognitive neuroscientist Dr. Jacob Jolij's research, Queen's 1970s hit "Don't Stop Me Now" was the top feel-good song of all time. Abba's Dancing Queen came in second place.

***

Baby rats are called kittens or pups. A group of rats is called a mischief.

***

The World's first and ancient university was established in Takshashila in 700 BC in India (modern day Pakistan). More than 10500 students from all over the world studied more than 60 subjects.

***

If you took out all of the empty space from between and within the atoms making up each human being, the entire human race would fit into the volume of a sugar cube.

***

The American Zoo Association has a "matchmaking site" known as the Population Management Center. It was started in June 2000 to help conserve species by facilitating matchmaking between zoos.

***

Alaska is both the Westernmost and Easternmost point of the United States. Alaska has an uninhabited Aleutian Island called Semisopochnoi which sits just 10 miles east of the 180th meridian.

***

Anatoli Brouchkov, a Russian geocryologist, injected himself with a 3.5-million-year-old strain of bacteria known as Bacillus F, which he found in a permafrost sample, just to see what would happen.

***

The highest point in Canada was only officially determined in 1992. An expedition finally reached the summit of Mount Logan and GPS put its elevation at 19,551 ft. Temperatures have been unofficially recorded at below -100F on the summit.

***

The North Island brown kiwi is a flightless, nocturnal bird that lays a single egg which averages 15% of its body size (about 1 lb.) It is the only bird known to consistently have both a left and right ovary as most birds have only a single ovary.

***

By the 1980's, Princess Marie Auguste of Anhalt, one of the last German princesses, was so broke she started a business adopting adult men and giving them the royal 'Prince' title in exchange for money. She made about 35 regular guys 'princes' and in the process made millions.

***

African grey parrots are highly social and recent research demonstrated they have evolved the ability to act selflessly. This is the first-time non-mammals have been observed helping each other in this way.

***

The Brookesia micra chameleon is believed to be the world's smallest at just over an inch long. It is found only on the small island of Nosy Hara, which is also home to the world's smallest lemur, giant lemurs, and the world's largest chameleons.

***

Israel is the only country in the world that has seen a net increase in trees over the last 100 years. Over that time frame, the Jewish National Fund has planted over 200 million trees.

***

Darwin's finches, which are a classic example of evolution, are dying off due to an infectious parasite that damages their beaks. The damage causes their mating calls to have an unpleasant tune, hindering their ability to reproduce.

***

In 1900, the Chinatown in Honolulu was intentionally burned down to prevent further spread of the bubonic plague. Four months after, Honolulu was deemed plague-free.

***

During the 1904 Summer Olympics in St. Louis, the American Frederick Lorz was the first to reach the finish line of the marathon race. It turned out, however, that he had covered about half the distance by car.

***

In 1787, Swiss scientific pioneer Horace Bénédict de Saussure cut off the top of Mont Blanc at 15,344 ft and it is now on display in the Teyler's museum in the Netherlands.

***

In 2001, the FBI warned Russell Crowe that al-Qaeda were planning to kidnap him as part of a "cultural destabilization plot." For nearly two years, the FBI guarded Crowe in public and refused to give him any details about the threat.

***

The 6 quarts of blood in the human body circulates through the body three times every minute. In one day, the blood travels a total ~12,000 miles - that's nearly half the circumference of Earth.

***

Thousands of years ago, people were performing a form of surgery called 'trepanation' that involves boring holes through a person's skull.

***

After Nike released the first Air Jordan sneakers in 1985, the NBA banned Michael Jordan from wearing them because its colors didn't match his team's uniform. Nike paid the per game fine of $5000 so he would continue wearing them.

***

In the 1840's, London's bus drivers had straps attached to their arms which ran alongside the bus that you tugged when you wanted to alert them to stop so you could alight.

***

In 2011, a monkey was arrested in Pakistan for crossing the border from India. The monkey was taken to Bahawalpur Zoo, where officials named him Bobby.

***

In WW2, there was a secret 1100-man US Army unit dubbed the 'Ghost Army', which was made up of artists, creatives & engineers. Their job was to create deceptions - from inflatable tanks to scripted bar conversations, their work led to big Allied wins.

***

The US was a signator of the Partial Test Ban Treaty, which prohibited all nuclear testing in the atmosphere, underwater and in outer space. However, in 1964 they conducted two underground nuclear tests in Mississippi which caused the earth to rise and roil in waves.

***

During the 7th century B.C., ancient Roman 'vestal virgins' were required to keep their hymens intact as proof of virginity until age 30 or they would be buried alive.

***

In 1970, an F-106 pilot engaging in mock combat lost control in a dive, ejected, and then the plane righted itself. It continued to fly and landed softly in a snowy field. The F-106 was later recovered with minimal damage and returned to service.

***

The World's first recorded labor strike was held during the building of the Great Pyramid of Giza in Egypt. The workers did not get their ration of garlic for the day and stopped working.

***

Norway sends ~5,000 teens each year to a refugee camp simulation for a day to help give them perspective. Nearly 100,000 teens have gone since the program started.

***

Robert Downey Jr. went from being paid $500,000 for playing Iron Man in the first Iron Man movie to making $50 million in the first The Avengers. His pay peaked at $80 million for Avengers: Age of Ultron.

***

In 1907, French waiters went on strike for the right to have mustaches. In France prior to 1907, mustaches were a symbol of class and stature, while waiters were seen as lower class and therefore not mustache-worthy.

***

In a recent study, scientists found that manta rays, which have the largest brain of all fish, show signs of recognizing themselves in the mirror and may be self-aware.

***

Former Yahoo CEO Marissa Mayer had a nursery built for her newborn in her office. This was at about the same time she stopped allowing parents and others to work from home.

***

Professional grade shuttlecocks are made only from the feathers of the left wing of geese. Feathers from the right wing make them spin the wrong way.

***

A 2013 study found that chewing gum boosts visual memory tasks and concentration. This study focused on the potential benefits of chewing gum during an audio memory task.

***

In 2009, Australian wallabies were getting into the medicinal opium fields and eating the poppies. They then hopped around while high resulting in crop circles.

***

A recent study found dogs and cats are ~25% more likely to get injured on the days surrounding a full moon, but no conclusive evidence as to why that is.

***

Vanilla is the second-most expensive spice after saffron because growing the vanilla seed pods is very labor-intensive. Pods are harvested daily to ensure the right maturity.

***

Male ants have no fathers because unfertilized ant eggs always produce male ants and only fertilized eggs produce female ants.

***

Immurement is a form of imprisonment, typically until death, in which a person is placed within an enclosed space with no exits. The prisoner eventually dies from starvation or dehydration.

***

During WW2, it was illegal in Britain to give cats a saucer of milk, dogs a biscuit, or bread to pigeons.

***

After his daily 20-km run in 1976, Shavarsh Karapetyan (a retired Armenian swimmer) came upon an accident scene where a bus had fallen into a reservoir. Repeatedly diving 10m deep, Karapetyan pulled 46 people out of the bus, 20 of whom survived.

***

Ninja's could tell time by how dilated a cat's pupils were as they dilate in a regular pattern throughout the day, regardless of ambient light.

***

Mr. P is a 101-year-old Italian man who survived both the Spanish Flu and WW2, and has now beat Covid-19 too. He was born in 1919 while the 1918 flu pandemic was raging in his hometown of Rimini.

***

Foxes use the Earth's magnetic field to estimate distances. It works as a kind of 'rangefinder', to estimate the distance to its prey and help them make a more accurate pounce.

***

The oldest continuously operating Chinese restaurant in the US is not in New York or San Francisco, but Butte, Montana. Pekin Noodle Parlor opened in 1911 and has been open ever since.

***

The male priapium fish (Phallostethus cuulong), which is named after the ancient Greek fertility deity Priapus, has its genitals right under its chin.

***

The Czech language was saved from extinction by puppet shows. In the 17th century, Catholic Ferdinand II forced the Protestant Czech's to speak in German and banned the Czech language. Puppets were the only thing with the right to speak Czech in public places.

***

Ancient Egyptians attempted to cure blindness by mixing mashed up pig's eyes, red clay, and honey which they then poured in the patient's ear.

***

Italian Frank Lentini was born in 1889 with a parasitic twin resulting in three legs, four feet, 16 toes and two genital organs. He earned his living as a circus artist named The Great Lentini.

***

Bats in the US eat so many insects (as much as their own body weight every day) that they save farmers an estimated $22.9 billion every year on pesticides.

***

Oxford University researchers found that when blindfolded, people have a difficult time identifying which toe is being poked, especially the two toes next to the big toe. This misidentification phenomenon is known as agnosia.

***

Singapore has a mandatory organ donation scheme (HOTA) for those >21 years of age. Anyone choosing to opt-out of donating their organs is given lower priority to receive an organ transplant if they ever find themselves in need.

***

In 1896, New York passed the Raines law to reduce Sunday drinking. The law had a loophole allowing bars to serve alcohol with a meal. Bars added an unappetizing Raines sandwich to every drink order, then took it away, serving it to the next customer. The sandwich often lasted weeks.

***

Sperm whales can reach a volume of up to 230 decibels with their songs, making them the loudest animal on Earth. For comparison, that is twice as loud as a jet taking off.

***

Anomia is the medical condition where individuals forget the names of common items or even proper names.

***

Will Wright got the inspiration for the original The Sims game while assessing his losses and material needs after his home burned down in the Oakland-Berkeley Firestorm.

***

Nelson Mandela's African birth name was Rolihlahla. In Xhosa, this literally translates to "pulling the branch of a tree" but more commonly translates to "troublemaker."

***

The world's oldest uneaten chocolates are over 100 years old. A tin of chocolates from the coronation of King Edward VII from 1902 sits in the St Andrews Preservation Trust Museum.

***

The world's longest treadmill is 7 feet wide by 30 feet long and started operating on August 26, 2011 at the Wolf Science Center in Ernstbrunn, Austria.

***

In 1970, a gay man discovered a loophole in Minnesota law that said gay marriage wasn't explicitly illegal, as long as officials allowed it. He then changed his name legally from 'Jack' to 'Pat Lyn', fooling officials and acquiring their marriage license.

***

In Ancient Rome, the punishment for killing one's father (parricide) was poena cullei or "penalty of the sack." This death penalty consisted of being sewn up in a sack along with a viper, a dog, and a cock, which was then thrown into water.

***

Being struck by lightning causes weird skin designs called 'Lichtenberg figures', named after the German physicist Georg Christoph Lichtenberg, who originally discovered and studied them.

***

Dogs evolved the specific (RAOL and LAOM) muscles that give them the ability to raise their inner eyebrows more than 33,000 years ago as they became domesticated. It's an evolutionary trick used to manipulate human emotions.

***

Ranald MacDonald, a bank clerk turned sailor, was the first English teacher in Japan. He taught 14 samurai English while he was held as prisoner.

***

The failure of the 1986 film "Howard the Duck" meant George Lucas had to sell some assets of Lucasfilm, including a computer-animated company Graphics Group to Steve Jobs. That company would go on to become Pixar.

***

In 1920, candy-maker Harry Burt created the first "ice cream on a stick" in Youngstown, Ohio. His first candy invention was called the Jolly Boy Sucker.

***

The Micronesian island of Yap is known for its stone money, known as Rai or Fei. They use large doughnut-shaped, carved disks of calcite, some as large as 13 ft in diameter. The rai is still used today for social transactions, such as marriage, inheritance, & political deals.

***

A mosquito's proboscis has six needles, two of which have 47 sharp edges on their tips to help cut through skin and even protective layers of clothing in order to suck your blood.

***

NASA's Office of Inspector General once raided a Denny's as part of a sting operation to bust a 75-year-old woman for possessing and attempting to sell a paperweight containing a moon rock the size of a rice grain.

***

Blue jeans originated in Genoa, Italy some 500 years ago. 'Bleu de Genes' were worn by fishermen and navy sailors because they could roll them up to prevent them getting wet and because they were easy to remove if they ever fell overboard.

***

There are lobsters who are not only colored differently but half their body is male and half is female. They are known as gynandromorphs.

***

On the Northwest tip of New Zealand's North island is 90 Mile Beach. The beach is officially a public highway but is only 55 miles long.

***

In Switzerland, applications for citizenship are decided at the municipal level. Thus, if your neighbors find you too annoying then they can vote to deny your citizenship.

***

Spain's S-80 submarine program designed subs that were 70 tons too heavy and likely to sink when submerged. The cost to fix it is expected to be ~$9 billion. The problem was traced back to an engineer misplacing a decimal point.

***

Per the 2017 census, only 12% of Qatar's population are Qatari citizens. The remaining 2.3 million people are expatriates.

***

The 'Rain of fish' is an annual event celebrated in the Honduran city of Yoro. During massive rain storms, hundreds of small silver fish supposedly rain from the sky onto the streets of the small town.

***

The wheel was not man's first significant invention. Others predate the wheel by thousands of years including sewing needles, woven cloth, rope, basket weaving, boats and even the flute.

***

Recent research has found that seals brought Tuberculosis to North & South America and not European explorers.

***

Iceland has one of the highest rates of legal gun ownership globally. The country has about 300,000 people and an estimated 90,000 guns. Interestingly enough, it also has one of the lowest rates of violent crime in the world.

***

During coronavirus related lockdown in the Netherlands, the National Institute for Public Health and the Environment recommended single people make arrangements with one other person as a cuddle/sex buddy.

***

The CEO of Juul himself has said in an interview that non-smokers should avoid vaping or using their Juul product as it's not intended for them and he also admits the long-term effects of vaping are unknown.

***

17-year-old English soldier Leonard Knight's life was saved by his pocket Bible when it stopped a German bullet during WWI. The bullet penetrated through to the last ~50 pages.

***

The Bahia emerald is a giant emerald from Brazil weighing over 800 lb. and containing 180,000 carats of precious gemstone. It has been at the center of an ownership dispute since 2008 and has an estimated worth of over $300 million.

***

Paul McCartney agreed to make a cameo on the TV show The Simpsons only if Lisa Simpson became a vegetarian for the rest of the series. The show agreed and he appeared in season 7 episode titled "Lisa the Vegetarian."

***

During WWII, the Allied's considered having a gardener inject estrogen into carrots to be eaten by Adolf Hitler in order to alter his hormones so he would become more feminine and less aggressive.

***

Researchers have found a male cheetah's "stutter" bark triggers the female reproductive system to release eggs. Unlike other cat species, female cheetahs lack a regular reproductive cycle and rarely ovulate.

***

During WW2, superstitious sailors in the navies would get a pig and a chicken tattooed on their feet to protect them from drowning.

***

In 1724, a Scottish woman was sentenced to be hanged, but she survived and the court ruled she couldn't be prosecuted further. She was given the nickname 'Half-Hangit Maggie' and lived for another 40 years.

***

New York City has the highest concentration of nesting Peregrine falcons in the world. They can soar over the city by taking advantage of updrafts from skyscrapers. The numerous pigeons are a constant food source which negates their need to migrate.

***

Older people who live in Hawaii have a higher life expectancy than the rest of the U.S. CDC research found residents older than 65 have an average life expectancy of 21.3 years. The average for all of the US was 19.1 years.

***

Before Colonel Harland Sanders started serving (Kentucky) fried chicken at his gas station cafe, he practiced law, delivered babies, sold both life insurance and car tires, and operated a steamboat ferry.

***

Zofia Rydet was a Polish photographer who, in 1978 at age 67, decided to try to shoot the interior of every home in Poland. Over the final 19 years of her life, she shot 20,000 images.

***

In the first two years of WWI, a broken leg meant an 80% chance of dying. Then the Thomas splint was introduced and reduced the rate of mortality down to 20%.

***

Termite queens have the longest lifespan of any insect in the world, living up to 50 years. Termites are also a delicacy in the diet of some human cultures and are often used in traditional medicines.

***

South Korean soccer team FC Seoul were fined a record 100 million Korean won after accidentally placing sex dolls instead of mannequins in their stands in the coronavirus aftermath.

***

As a result of a 2007 partnership with the USPS, NYC's Saks Fifth Avenue flagship store's 8,500 sq. ft. shoe department has its own zip code: 10022-SHOE.

***

Every 3 years, Ypres Belgium has a cat parade called Kattenstoet, culminating in stuffed animals being thrown from the bell tower. It originates from the middle ages, where they threw live feral cats from the tower on "Cats Wednesday".

***

During the Ottoman Empire, male heirs were locked in a part of the Imperial palace called kafes ("the cage"). They lived under guard and house arrest unless they succeeded the throne. This was to avoid a war of succession and ensure the survival of the royal dynasty.

***

The tradition of pouring out some of your drink on the ground to show respect for deceased friends or family comes from an ancient practice known as libation. It was common in ancient Egypt, Greece, and Rome.

***

Ruperts were dummy paratroopers dropped by Allied forces away from the actual Normandy invasion site on D-Day to try and divert German troops. They were designed to burst into flames on landing to avoid detection.

***

The most common street name in the U.S. is Second St. First is the third most common street name, Third is the second most common, while Fifth is the sixth most common.

***

The 2018 'slapping law' in Russia decriminalized some forms of domestic violence. If it is a first offense and not enough to hospitalize them, then instead of 2 years in jail the offender pays a minimum fine of 5 rubles (or less than $1).

***

Vatican officials tasked with finding Latin words for modern English words have translated the internet to inter rete and emails to inscriptio cursus electronici.

***

A Russian 3D bioprinter successfully produced beef, rabbit, and fish tissue on the International Space Station using magnetic fields in microgravity.

***

When Lady Gaga was studying at NYU, her classmates made a Facebook group called "Stefani Germanotta, you will never be famous" where they bullied her. She dropped out after only a year to pursue her music career full time.

***

The Spanish ribbed newt, when attacked, pushes out its ribs until they pierce through its body, exposing a row of bones that act like poisonous barbs. The behavior doesn't have any long-term harmful effects on the newt itself.

***

Garfield phones have been washing up on Northern Finistere beaches in France for over 30 years. A shipping container fell off the cargo ship in a storm and ended up wedged in a nearby underwater cave.

***

The Northern Scorpion, Canada's only scorpion, can have as many as 12 eyes but they are mainly light-sensitive and only able distinguish light from dark. However, they are so sensitive they can actually navigate by the stars at night.

***

Statistically speaking, the most dangerous job in America is President. Roughly 9% have been killed while in office.

***

Sea urchins got their name from hedgehogs, which until about the 15th century were called "urchins." Therefore, sea urchins are basically ocean hedgehogs.

***

In New Zealand, then 16-year-old Adrian Mann built one of the world's largest grand pianos, which he named the Alexander Piano. It is almost 19 feet long and weighs ~1.2 tons.

***

There are people who suffer delusions that they are made of different materials, including glass or cement. French King Charles VI was one of the most notable sufferers of "glass delusion."

***

The TV series Hannibal had a cinematic shot of a naked flayed couple. NBC thought this was unacceptable because their buttcracks were showing. The director offered to fill their buttcracks with blood to make it less offensive. NBC allowed the shot with that modification.

***

The 'Happy Birthday' song was not legally available for public use until a 2016 lawsuit settlement. Until then, it was copyrighted and you had to pay a license to use it.

***

Entomologists and other scientists use a simple device called a pooter to carefully pick up live insects.

***

More Guinness is consumed in Nigeria, which consumes the second most globally behind only the UK, than in Ireland. Guinness has been sold in Nigeria since 1827. The United States consumes the fourth most Guinness worldwide.

***

Newborn babies were given mini face shields during the Coronavirus COVID-19 disease outbreak in Bangkok, Thailand.

***

Tom Brady is selling his customized stretch Escalade for $300,000. There are five back seats under a raised roof, including two VIP electric recliners with hand veneered burl wood folding tables. It has ~13,000 miles on the odometer.

***

Charges were dropped against Australian activist Danny Lim for displaying the word "cunt" on a public sandwich board after the appeals judge ruled the word is "prevalent in everyday language" in Australia.

***

Healthcare workers are taping photos of themselves to their PPE to help put COVID-19 patients at ease. They believe that giving patients hope through a friendly face is half the battle.

***

Ian Martin was hired as a swearing consultant for BBC's political comedy series The Thick Of It. The script would be sent to Ian to add more "colorful language."

***

In 2011, the Supreme Court of India opened six of the seven secret vaults of Padmanabhaswamy Temple and discovered $22 billion in treasure including golden idols, golden elephants, 18-foot diamond necklaces, as well as countless bags of gold coins.

***

A Brazilian doctor used 3d printing to help blind parents feel their baby's ultrasound. Dr. Werner uses a 3D printer to make lifelike models from images obtained by a GE ultrasound machine.

***

Whorehouse Meadow, a meadow near Frenchglen, Oregon, was renamed in the 1960's to "Naughty Girl Meadow" on the Bureau of Land Management maps. The old name was restored in 1981 after public outcry.

***

In 2015, Dwayne 'The Rock' Johnson captured the world record for the most selfies taken in 3 minutes with 105 snaps at the world premiere of his movie San Andreas. The record is currently at 168.

***

At least 43 buildings in New York City, like the General Motors and Empire State Buildings, have their own zip code due to their sheer size or amount of people who work there.

* * *

According to the World Meteorological Society, Yuma, Arizona receives over 4,000 hours of sunlight annually, which is the most of any city in the world. On a given day, there is a 90% chance of sunshine.

* * *

A recent study by researchers at the University of St. Andrews found that migrating humpback whales could be linked to their origin region by their whale songs. Each region and population of whales has their own unique songs.

* * *

The first commercially successful videotape recorder, precursor to the VCR, was made in 1956 and was the size of a piano. The Ampex Corporation developed the VRX-1000 in 1956 and sold it to TV networks and stations for $50,000.

* * *

The word "hangover" first appeared in the English vocabulary in the 19th century as a term for describing "unfinished business" from meetings, but it was not until 1904 that the word began to be used in relation to alcohol.

* * *

A 3000-year-old Egyptian sarcophagus lid was found hidden in the walls of a British man's home. It was discovered by an auctioneer who was sorting through the house after the man died.

***

A slave, Nathan "Nearest" Green, originally taught Jack Daniels how to make whiskey and is now credited as their first master distiller.

***

After every tea Alfred Hitchcock finished on set, he would throw the tea cup and saucer over his shoulder allowing them to shatter on the ground.

***

There is a small rock island, Ilha da Queimada Grande, off the coast of Southern Brazil that is home to roughly 1 snake per square meter.

***

In Denmark, there are some traffic signals with small Viking figures.

***

One of the earliest recipes for ice cream, or icy cream as it was called in this 1660's recipe, included ambergreece/ambergris or whale feces for flavoring.